Wilkes Booth Came to Washington

LARRY STARKEY

RANDOM HOUSE   NEW YORK

Copyright © 1976 by Larry K. Starkey

All rights reserved under International
and Pan-American Copyright Conventions.
Published in the United States by Random House, Inc.,
New York, and simultaneously in Canada by Random House
of Canada Limited, Toronto.

Library of Congress Cataloging in Publication Data

Starkey, Larry, 1942–
Wilkes Booth came to Washington.

Bibliography: p.
Includes index.
1. Lincoln, Abraham, Pres. U.S., 1809–1865—Assassination.   2.   Booth, John Wilkes, 1838–1865.   I.   Title.
E457.5.S78   364.1'524   76–14172
ISBN 0-394-48894-6

Manufactured in the United States of America

2 4 6 8 9 7 5 3

First Edition

*Wilkes Booth
Came to Washington*

This book, with all of my love,
is dedicated to five people,

Bethany
Rebecca
Daniel

... in the hope they will remember
that it is more important to raise questions
than to find answers.

Gail

... and "Mizpah"

Wilkes Booth came to Washington,
An actor great was he;
He played at Ford's Theatre,
And Lincoln went to see.

—CONTEMPORARY SONG

CONTENTS

FOREWORD
page viii

CHAPTER I
Introduction to the Play
page 3

CHAPTER II
North of the North
page 14

CHAPTER III
Border Incidents
page 28

CHAPTER IV
"Wilkes Booth Came to Washington..."
page 44

CHAPTER V
A Small Company of Irregulars
page 61

CHAPTER VI
The Last Days of the Lost Cause
page 72

CHAPTER VII
The Ultimate Border Incident
page 80

CHAPTER VIII
"Long Live Our Chief, the President"
page 87

CHAPTER IX
The Secretary's Medicine
page 103

CHAPTER X
"Hail to the Chief . . ."
page 113

CHAPTER XI
"The Midnight Special"
page 120

CHAPTER XII
Running Away on One Leg
page 129

CHAPTER XIII
The Missing Link
page 150

CHAPTER XIV
Postmortem
page 169

Bibliography
page 191

Notes
page 199

Index
page 205

FOREWORD

THIS BOOK BEGAN many years ago in one of those late-summer pestilences which Washingtonians try to pass off as merely "a heat wave." I left my home—then in Arlington County, Virginia—early on such a weekend morning to retrace Wilkes Booth's escape route.

Newly arrived in Washington with an academic background in American history and an assistant editor's job on a company magazine, I was filling most of my spare time either loving my newborn daughter or visiting the remnants of our national collective past with which Washington abounds.

On the maps Wilkes' route appears to have a purposeful direction, working a more or less straight line toward the south. But as I drove from one stopover to another, and checked distances against his known arrival and departure times, it began to appear that this was a desperate rather than a calcu-

Foreword / ix

lated escape route. My first reaction to this was to wonder why a man would kill the President of the United States without first preparing an escape plan. My second was to recall that he had broken his leg in jumping from Lincoln's box to the stage of Ford's Theatre—and my third was to ask myself a question I could not answer at that time: Where was he planning to escape to, before the broken leg thwarted his plans?

This book is based on the answer to that question and many others. It is not meant to stand as the last word about the conspiracy to assassinate Abraham Lincoln. It proposes a thesis because the facts which answer the many questions raised by the assassination point to that thesis. But there is no startling new information in the pages that follow—though much of the information has not previously been published in the context of the assassination—and there are no hitherto-undisclosed revelations. What follows are facts answering such questions as the one I asked myself that muggy afternoon ten years ago.

The answers, wherever possible, have come from original sources—and these have included thousands of pages of trial transcripts covering a military tribunal, a civil murder trial and a presidential impeachment, as well as Lincoln's own papers and the diaries of his contemporaries. The curious reader, for that matter, may find the bibliography particularly frustrating, since some sources exist only as rare old editions.

Secondary sources have included histories based upon interviews with those who participated in forming the times with which this story is involved, and others based upon unquestionable scholarship. The bibliography for these is less frustrating, though in some cases it includes books that have been out of print for many decades.

Finally, to make certain that Author's Myopia wasn't setting in, during the research a careful effort was made to weigh every Lincoln assassination theory, no matter how dubious, against the developing information. Throughout the text, an effort has been made to provide footnotes where others have proposed alternative interpretations of the same material, and in some cases where I believe different interpretations could be drawn, along with the reasons supporting my own conclusions.

THIS BOOK DOES, however, have a bias. There has been a very conscious attempt to write it with an understanding of the times during which the events it describes transpired.

For while it is true that the research is hewn from texts, the narrative is constructed upon footwork.

I can remember standing under the giant sycamore tree which Thomas Lincoln once planted in Kentucky, and which today casts large shadows over the marble memorial encasing the tiny log cabin that legend identifies as Abe Lincoln's birthplace. Lincoln wrote of the bears and wolves that were a part of his childhood, and it is next to that sycamore that a twentieth-century person can try to understand being ten years old in 1822.

In Springfield, Illinois, where Lincoln had enjoyed local fame as a lawyer, I've wondered, looking about the parlor where he received the official delegation informing him he was President-elect of the United States, about the times in which a man whose immediate ancestors had been killed by Indians could be called to such an office.

I've seen, as well, many of the sights his life was governed by. In Charleston, South Carolina, I've walked the length of the old slave market. Its claustrophobic stone and steel cells terrify even a free man now, and history books that tell of the days when it was filled with humanity from slave-ship holds cannot convey the atrocious reality of it. At Gettysburg, Pennsylvania, I've studied the line of Pickett's infamous charge, walked the grass of it, and in my mind's eye tried to understand the feelings of the 15,000 men who marched out over it that day in 1863. And I've tried to understand what the half of them, straggling back a half-hour later, meant by their tears and curses. Outside of Fredericksburg, Virginia, I leaned against the stone wall on the mountain base where the slaughter of Union soldiers sent uselessly against entrenched Confederate batteries didn't deter General Burnside from sending more and more of them until the bodies lay six feet deep. That is lost humanity nearly as tall as I am, wasted in a commander's determination to win.

In Ford's Theatre, I've reenacted the positions of all the parties during the shooting of President Lincoln, and since that first time I've retraced Wilkes' so-called escape route a total of three times.

I've watched that haunted play, *Our American Cousin*, turning my head upwards and to the right at the fateful lines. And listened to it, over and again.

I've even stood, exactly one hundred years to the day and the hour after the President's death, outside the Peterson House in a cold April rain and tried to feel what the men felt a century before as they left that ugly little room of death and stepped out into a similar rain. I tried to think of them, and of the bureaucrat who added into his daily record of the day's weather, "President Lincoln died today."

Many times I've stood alone before Abraham Lincoln's grave, trying to comprehend this genius, this sixteenth President of the United States, this man. I've been there before and after witnessing such places as Antietam, Chattanooga, Appomattox, Atlanta, Manassas Junction, Perryville, Staunton River Bridge, the Shenandoah Valley, Harper's Ferry, Richmond, Charleston, Petersburg, and many more. I've visited all of them, trying all the while to understand this very great man, Lincoln, within the context of the times *he* knew.

I have tried to do the same with his assassin. And it is Wilkes Booth, after all, who is the subject of this book. And I must confess that in all the years of research, I've grown to like him—much as, along with every American, I must detest the shot he fired.

John Wilkes Booth murdered a man whom I believe to have been the finest President these United States have seen. He paid for that crime with his life—and hopefully I will be forgiven for treating kindly this very decent and young man who felt obligated to do what he believed a patriot should do.

The story which follows constitutes a marshaling of certain facts within the context that the people responsible for creating those facts knew. History is not a mass process in which individuals are important only as droplets support a wave. History is individual human beings acting upon information available *at that moment* rather than after it.

This book is a very conscious effort to interpret and to organize and to relate known facts in the contemporary setting of the people who made those facts a reality. And as you read this book, it is important to remember that war exists where law—where the orderly adjudication of human differences—has ceased to function.

The events which follow in this text are from such a period.

THERE ARE PEOPLE who deserve thanks for this book, even as I'll deservedly take the lumps for any flaws. My father is first among them. During the late 1930's he began broadcasting five days a week over NBC from coast to coast, weaving stories of Western history that were meticulous in their facts and enthralling in their presentation. Dad recognized that history itself is drama, requiring no distortion—and this is intended to be a book he would have enjoyed. And approved of.

A lot of years ago, I went to work at a newspaper for a man named Hal Neitzel. I am obligated to him for a good deal more than an introduction to the works of Thomas Wolfe, though that would have been enough. Along with Robert Loomis, who insists upon a clarity and logic of language—and who, through sheer belief that such is possible, does make it happen—Hal Neitzel has encouraged a rhythm of language and a precision of phrase which is hopefully reflected in the pages which follow.

Three of the people to whom this book is dedicated are, as this is written, children. Each of them in many ways has reminded me of how a learning mind must be an open mind—following facts and logic and whatever to a conclusion, and from that conclusion to new learning. I hope, very much, that when they are adults this book will remind them of that lesson.

AT THE END, there is a warm and gentle and incisive critic named Gail. The fact that the book is done at all is due to her.

Manhattan, Springtime, 1976

CHAPTER

I

Introduction to the Play

SOMEWHERE OFF BY THE MARSHES near the railroad bridge, a lone steam engine blew its whistle into the not yet fully born dawn. Pitched to the final tone of a dirge, the note traveled slow and hesitant through the nightmist draping the Potomac's smooth rivertop, and, somewhere among the sandstone columns of the Capitol Building, it dimmed at last in a hushed *sanglot*. The President was dying.

THE DOCTORS, searching for his wounds, had stripped the formal black coat from his massive shoulders as he lay barely breathing inside Ford's Theatre. Now, as the soldiers used fixed bayonets to clear the crowds in their path, it covered his chest like a blanket as the volunteer litter-bearers carried his limp body across the sloshing mud of 10th Street.

Each of the doctors had examined him as he lay upon the

floor of the Presidential Box, his bloodied head cradled in the lap of the actress, Laura Keene, and each in his turn had proclaimed that the wounds would kill him. But when mortal skills fail, few men deny miracles. And so, knowing the President must be moved to quarters where they could care for him, and knowing he could not possibly survive the trip to the White House, they carried him out of the theatre, not knowing where they would set him down.

Slipping in the mud of the unpaved street, dodging to the left and the right as the confused and hysterical mob surged about them, they drifted generally in the direction of a solitary man on a porch who held a lantern aloft and shouted, "Here! Bring him here!"

Inside, they tossed the coat unceremoniously into a corner, and on top of it dropped the urine-soaked trousers as soon as they could slip them from his legs. Throughout the night, as doctors and mourners and officials came and went, the suit which had been tailor-made for his second Inauguration just six weeks earlier lay quietly wrinkling in the corner while mustard plasters replaced clothing as a covering for the President's body.

A LIGHT RAIN shrouded the dawn which came to dim the gas jet in that little tenement-house room on 10th Street into which were crowded most of the leaders of the United States. Shortly afterwards, at a little past seven o'clock, the President's breathing suddenly became labored and staccato. He choked upon the drop of brandy the doctors forced between his lips, rallied a little, and then sank back into what was obviously his final agony. Dr. Charles Leale, remembering from battlefield experience that the mortally wounded sometimes regain consciousness at the moment of death, sat at the President's side and took hold of his hand so that he would know he was among friends, and Surgeon-General Barnes readied his pocket watch to record the exact moment of death.

Introduction to the Play / 5

In another room, Secretary of the Interior John Usher was asleep on an unmade bed; four blocks away Vice President Andrew Johnson tossed uncertainly in his own bed at the Kirkwood Hotel, and some would later claim he had relied on strong drink to calm his shattered nerves. Most of the other members of the government surrounded either the bloodstained bed where the President lay or the little table nearby where Secretary of War Edwin M. Stanton continued dictating orders to the police, to his secret detectives, and to the million men-at-arms under his direct command. Soon, as Surgeon-General Barnes' watch ticked on, Stanton ceased his dictation and took his place at the bedside of his President and his closest friend. At twenty-two minutes past the morning hour of seven, the irregular sound of the President's breathing ceased. Stanton stood for a moment in silence, then with absent-minded nervousness and grief first put his hat on his head and immediately afterwards removed it. Then into the silence of that unlikely deathroom he uttered what many would remember as "Now he belongs to the ages."*

Dr. Charles Taft, who like Dr. Leale had visited Ford's that evening for relaxation, rose from his wooden chair beside the cheap little bed, his long night's labors ended, his knowledge useless, his skills no longer needed. The still-warm body of his unexpected patient, now no more than a figure in a grotesque still life, lay stretched diagonally before him, the two death-coins holding shut his eyes.

The room—too small to hold the many who had been there through the night—was filled now with too much exhaled breath, and too much smell of tension's sweat. It was a dirty little room in which to die, stuck in the back of a brick tenement house and connected to the front of that house by a

---

* In some accounts written either by Stanton's enemies or by his enemies' biographers, his eloquence is disputed. Apparently, a good many of those present felt he had said, "Now he belongs to the angels." The version quoted is the most likely—and certainly the one Lincoln himself would have preferred.

narrow hallway through which Dr. Taft passed before opening the front door and stepping into a cold April rain. Across 10th Street from the low brick porch upon which he stood was Ford's New Theatre, with soldiers now patrolling in front of its locked doors, and six blocks west of it Tad Lincoln slept fitfully in the White House, waking less frequently to sob now than when he had first been told of it the night before.

Surrounding the little open-top brick porch were springtime's lilacs, and as the cold rain assaulted Dr. Taft's wearied body, he inhaled their fresh and light scent. "When lilacs last in the door-yard bloom'd," Walt Whitman would later sing of that morning: ". . . I mourn'd, and yet shall mourn with ever-returning spring."

Dr. Taft would spend the rest of his life reminding friends that he could never afterwards smell lilacs without feeling a sense of nausea. A nation that had been so high with victory only the morning before had now sunk so low as this mourning. Abraham Lincoln, surrounded by his legions and his cheering people, was dead in his own capital city, his skull cracked open by a murderer's bullet.

FOR MORE THAN A CENTURY following that terrible morning, generation after generation of American schoolchildren have learned the same story: The demented actor John Wilkes Booth put together a little band of ne'er-do-well Southern sympathizers, shot the President, and was later killed while seeking shelter in Virginia among Confederates so horrified at his crime that they refused him assistance. It is a story that is not only unsupported by the facts, but one which runs directly contrary to most of the known facts. Wilkes was in fact helped by virtually every Southerner he contacted during his flight; there is little evidence that his co-conspirators were recruited by Wilkes himself—and much evidence that he, like the others, was recruited by the real masterminds behind the crime; far from being a demented and unknown actor, Wilkes Booth was

Introduction to the Play / 7

wealthy and famous, and was known to his acquaintances as a warm and friendly and talented young man.

Wilkes Booth is in many ways a disappointing villain of American history. For the President's own greatness in his office, his very deep personal humility and abiding faith in the Republic, almost requires his murderer to be the most base and evil of men. It is not to our discredit as a people that we would prefer a history filled with evil and pure antagonists, with the former—through brutality and chicanery—sometimes winning temporary victories, but with truth and right always triumphing in the end. We want to read such history while leading our own confusing and insecure lives as we envy those few statesmen who control our affairs with an unfailing wisdom to which most of us are not privy.

The problem is that history is a sloppy and accidental process, with fallible men making decisions based on emotion as often as on logic, and being right only about as often as they are wrong, if that often. God knows we would all be fools of the highest order if we did not pray for political leaders of infallible wisdom and judgment; otherwise we are left entrusting mere mortals with the power to drag us into foolish wars, destroy our economies, play with our liberties, and in short, through caprice or misjudgment or simple damnfoolishness, ruin with the stroke of a pen those private worlds of homes and families we have struggled lifetimes to build.

We should indeed pray for such men in our futures. But we cannot afford the luxury of viewing our history with such high hopes for its nobility. For if history holds any value at all, it is in its ability to teach us the consequences of our mistakes.

It has become fashionable since 1963 to seek conspiracies behind the assassinations of public men, despite commissions of public officials and juries of our peers finding that individuals acted alone out of madness to deprive us of charismatic and vital leaders. The reason for the continued skepticism is that neither the commissions nor the juries have provided us with full and complete answers. They have given us the answers which supported theories of demented individuals lashing out against our national leaders for personal reasons. But there are questions involved in each of these modern assassinations which are not answered by theories based exclusively on demented individuals—and so we seek more than a single assassin; we seek a conspiracy of men, a group which met and planned to kill a national leader. We do so not because the numbers involved in such a murder are important, but because the fact of such a conspiracy must involve at least a reason why those involved came together. It is that reason, that motive, that is important to us—because, if the motive exists, then in order to avoid a repetition of the tragedy we must know what caused it.

In the case of the murder of Abraham Lincoln, such a conspiracy did exist, and we have ignored it for more than a century. But assume for a moment that the school version is correct and that John Wilkes Booth was demented and did in fact shoot Abraham Lincoln only because of his insanity. Consider whether or not that version provides adequate answers to the following questions:

> —At the same time President Lincoln was shot, an accomplice of Booth's attempted to murder the Secretary of State, William Seward. No attempt was made on the life of any other official of the government.* Why was Seward made the target?
> —Wilkes Booth was certain to be recognized when he jumped to the stage after shooting the President, since he was a particularly popular actor at Ford's Theatre. Why did he wear no disguise?

* It has been believed that assassins were sent after General Grant, Vice President Johnson, and Secretary of War Stanton. As will be demonstrated later, there were other reasons for curious actions regarding the first two men, and the "assassin" assigned to Stanton amounted to no more than a suspicious shadow which a panicky aide thought he had seen lurking about the War Secretary's home after the President was murdered.

Introduction to the Play / 9

—When he was asked to identify himself by the guard at the Anacostia Bridge, Booth gave his correct name even though an accomplice who was only minutes behind him gave an alias. Why did Booth give his correct name?
—Nearly a year before he killed President Lincoln, Booth gave up a stage career which by his mid-twenties had made him wealthy and famous. Why?
—After killing the President, Booth rode directly to a pre-arranged rendezvous in Maryland, where he picked up a rifle and met an accomplice. But, having broken his leg, he was forced to find a doctor—after which he appeared to wander from shelter to shelter with no plan of escape going farther than the next hiding place to which various Confederate sympathizers could take him. What escape route was he planning to take if his leg had not been broken?

The insanity theory is largely useless to us in answering such questions. But there are answers to them. And all of the answers involve Montreal, in Canada.

There, on the morning Abraham Lincoln died, at least a score of men holding Confederate commissions had been heard for the last week to speak of "good news coming soon from Washington."

It was a hurried plot—less than a week old—and a desperate one. They had sent the brilliant and famous actor John Wilkes Booth to fire a soft-lead derringer ball into the President's skull. Now they waited for word of his success—and for him. Much as none of them would shed a tear for Lincoln's lost life, still that was not the real object of their efforts; now it was necessary for the assassin to escape to them in Canada.

THE PLOT HAD BEGUN only a bit more than a week earlier when the chief courier between Montreal and Richmond—young John Harrison Surratt, Jr.—had arrived from the Confederate capital with the chilling news that Jefferson Davis and the rest of their government had fled Richmond. Surratt had met with the Confederate Secretary of State, Judah P. Benjamin, only the day before the evacuation.

President Davis was calling for guerrilla warfare after Richmond's fall—calling for all Southerners to strike in the night and fade away at dawn. No longer having land to defend, the Southern leader was calling for indiscriminate warfare-by-stealth.

Such extraordinary duties had been the mission of the Confederate agents in Montreal since Secretary of State Benjamin had first sent them to Canada a year earlier—to strike with guerrillas across the international border in order to create war between the United States and Canada. And so it would not be difficult for them to create a scenario that would send Booth against Lincoln.

In that imaginary playlet, the President of the United States has been assassinated, and the Secretary of State as well. The murderer has fled to Canada, and from there it is made known that Confederate agents in Montreal are responsible for the crime. The newspapers in the Union report the facts, and the population of the Union cries out for vengeance.

Federal troops are already in Buffalo and Detroit, stationed there in earlier days to prevent further Confederate border incidents. And now public pressure forces the new President, Andrew Johnson—a Southerner himself—to issue new orders to these troops. Federal gunboats converge on the Great Lakes at both of these port cities and begin to board troops. As the gunboats are crossing toward the Canadian beachhead, additional troops are crossing the Maine and Vermont borders.

Some weeks of confusion follow, and there are skirmishes every now and again as the limited English forces fight a delaying action. Finally, Britain launches its attack—the armadas arrive, and heavily gunned men-of-war begin shelling Boston

Introduction to the Play / 11

Common, New York City, Baltimore. For the second time in half a century, Washington itself comes under English attack.*

Union troopers are pulled by the thousands from Grant's command in Virginia to defend the North itself, leaving Sherman stranded in the Carolinas. Paroled Confederate veterans spit quietly into the dust in their farmyards, then tear up the pledges they have signed in order to return to their lands rather than enter Union prison camps, and begin marching to join Johnston or Lee again. Along the way, deserters, with renewed hearts, join them.

Sherman and Grant each find increased guerrilla activity along their flanks, and must tighten their defenses. Dependent upon forage to feed his army, Sherman finds ambushes waiting for his foragers.

On the Mexican border, Maximilian† sends a worrying force against the U.S. troops stationed there, and in the process finds himself in a cooperative military expedition with forces under the command of Confederate General Kirby Smith.

Grant, now fully occupied with protecting the Northern cities

---

* This is the scenario as the Canadian Confederates could have imagined it. Unknown to them, however, were sealed orders given to the English fleet commander in the Atlantic requiring him to take precisely such action in the event a Union army entered Canadian territory. There is, moreover, ample evidence that many English government and military officials did not doubt that such orders would be activated by some incident before the Civil War's end.

† Maximilian, the French puppet dictator in Mexico, had in fact been advised by the Confederates that Lincoln proposed to them during December 1864 that the Civil War end so an expedition could be made against Mexico. Doubtless, the Davis government passed the same information to its cabal in Canada. It was common knowledge in every capital that as soon as the Confederacy was subdued, a Union force would enter Mexico to assist the nationalist leader, Juarez, in defeating Maximilian. No lower an official than Ulysses S. Grant—privy to conversations on the subject of Mexico with President Lincoln before the assassination—would, as soon as he could spare the troops from fighting rebels, dispatch a major force under the command of celebrated cavalry commander General Philip Sheridan to be in a position to move against Maximilian as soon as the invasion orders could be issued. With Sheridan's help, Juarez ultimately stood Maximilian before a firing squad.

from the English fleet, and with the necessity of reinforcing the invasion forces against Canada, is helpless to prevent Lee's army from moving directly south along the railroad between Danville, Virginia, and Columbia, North Carolina, to hit Sherman from the north as Johnston punches away at the Union belly from the south.

British supply ships—joined by the French—begin arriving in Southern port cities as rapidly as the Union forces are driven from them. In the holds of these ships are arms, ammunition, food, clothing, and medical supplies. Fresh British and French troops are landed as the paroled Confederate soldiers begin rejoining their old regiments.

Jefferson Davis, in a temporary headquarters at Danville, signs his name to a military alliance with the two superpowers within days of their own separate declarations of war against the United States. The new President, Andrew Johnson, faced with a three-front war, blockades of his main ports, and renewed pressure from the peace elements in the Union itself, is forced to dispatch emissaries to treat with the heads of the three other governments.

To French Mexico is returned California and that portion of the Southwest, not including Texas, which the United States took following the Mexican War in 1846. The English claims for the return of the Northwest—Washington State and Oregon —must be accepted. Recognition of the Confederate States of America as an independent and sovereign nation is perhaps the hardest pill of all, but that, too, the United States must swallow.

SUCH WAS THE HEADY WINE being served up around the bar of the Queen's Hotel. Remember that we are here considering only what desperate men might fantacize *could* happen, not what *would* have happened—but even at that, more rational heads than the Confederate exiles, worn upon the shoulders of high-ranking diplomats in London and Paris and Washington, did in fact imagine similar scenarios. And it is a scenario not unlike the one following the assassination at Sarejevo in 1914 which began World War I.

It sounds absurd—and for that matter, it was—but to understand it requires a comprehension of the times and the politics and the emotions of 1865 . . . times of upheaval, politics of uncertainty, and emotions such as are aroused only by the tugs and tensions of fratricidal warfare.

CHAPTER

II

North of the North

AMERICA, BEFORE 1860, had been the nation envisioned by Thomas Jefferson, a country in which the President of the United States walked among his fellow citizens as an equal whose job made him their servant. Before 1860 the President traveled freely among his countrymen, without guards, and lived in a house that did not need to be separated from them by a fence.

For that matter, during his tenure in the White House, Abraham Lincoln never experienced the convenience of a toilet that could be flushed. Washington was a city of dirt streets and board sidewalks in which employees of the British embassy drew extra tropical-duty pay because of the high incidence of malaria, and a city in which red-light districts competed with saloons for the salaries of the soldiers and bureaucrats who lived there. The Washington Monument stood at half its current height, and the great dome of the Capitol Building—which had been begun under the leadership of then Secretary of War Jefferson Davis—was still uncompleted. In the building itself were huge bakeries making bread for the soldiers camped about the city, and along Pennsylvania Avenue between the Capitol and the White House, rooming houses faced one another across a street that was dusty and mosquito-laden in the dry months and soggy and mosquito-laden in the wet months. "Nice" people walked only on the north side of Pennsylvania Avenue, where the rooming houses did not feature quarters furnished with prostitutes and where gamblers and thieves did not flourish.

Just off Pennsylvania Avenue, at its intersection with 12th Street, was the Kirkwood Hotel, where Andrew Johnson lived; two blocks closer to the White House was Willard's Hotel, where Julia Howe wrote "The Battle Hymn of the Republic" and, near it, the street where "Newspaper Row" housed all of the reporters of the important papers. At 15th Street was the Treasury Building, and looking back down along Pennsylvania Avenue from it to Capitol Hill a person could see the main street of the nation, bisected by trolley tracks and filled alternately with livestock vendors hawking their sheep or cattle or chickens to the city's few housewives, or their sin-peddling counterparts hawking other livestock to soldiers and congressmen.

In the White House, most days a person could wander at will everywhere on the grounds and in the mansion itself except for that portion of it set off as the private quarters of the President—a small apartment on the second floor of the East Wing. Seeing the President didn't even require a prior appointment if the visitor didn't mind standing in line for a while and maybe having to buy a lemonade from the counter Tad Lincoln set up every so often in the lobby.

The park directly across the avenue from the White House was still mostly famous as the place where an aging congressman shot Francis Scott Key's nephew after several warnings had not deterred the young man from the intimacy he enjoyed with the congressman's youthful bride. South of the White House was "Murder Bay," a slum section built on top of the Potomac swamp and separated by Ohio Avenue from the section called "Hooker's Division." The name became synonymous with the profession of the female residents.

Going back along the river toward the Capitol required passing the livestock pastures and the fish stalls which produced the odors that were the primary reason why there was seldom a jam-up of shoppers, and also the reason why President Lincoln vacated the city as often as possible during the summer months to take respite in private quarters at a place called "The Soldier's Home." Closer still to the Capitol was the deep water of the swamp into which the corpses of countless army horses, cattle and mules (and God knows how many unfortunate adventurers from "Murder Bay") were dumped.

The American capital was essentially an army camp in 1865—and one to be shunned as an unpleasant cesspool by foreign diplomats accustomed to more pleasant working conditions. To a European aristocrat, it was every horrible imagining of republican life suddenly brought into reality—ranging from the lack of amenities to the familiarity with which Americans treated their elected officials.

And Americans treated few elected officials quite as familiarly as they treated Abraham Lincoln. In the spring of 1864, few Americans—north or south—viewed him without strong opinions. And many in the North joined the majority in the South in a special loathing for the President of the United States.

By the spring of 1864, scant months before the presidential elections, Southern fortunes were not yet bleak. Rebel forces knew they had been in a fight—which was something they had not expected back in '61—but the seceding states had held their borders more or less solid throughout the war. Northern

Unionists had to view their President as a man who had not only begun the war, but as the man who had failed to win it; after three years of bloodshed, the Union—in the spring of 1864—had shown no demonstrable success. True enough, the South was beaten—but that is an historian's analysis, not an 1864 contemporary's assessment. To the citizens of the North halfway into 1864, the Lincoln government had failed to win the war it had made necessary. Lincoln, the Illinois lawyer whose opponents in 1860 had promised the country a disaster if he was elected, had proven his enemies to be prophets.

It was a bad position for a President to be in during an election year. But the presidential election of 1864 was a curious one. The candidates were the President of the United States —the Commander-in-Chief of the military forces—and, against him, the man who had been his chief general throughout most of the Civil War—Union General George Brinton McClellan. Lincoln had replaced McClellan as his chief combat officer after McClellan had failed to win the war, and now the former general was running as a peace candidate. It was a nip-and-tuck election—so much so that Lincoln himself felt compelled to write a note intended only for his own eyes, to remind himself that he must find a way to end the war between Election Day and the Inauguration of his own successor.

The opponents of Lincoln had plenty of fodder to feed upon. The President of the United States was in command of 1,062,000 well-fed, well-trained troops, equipped with the most advanced means of delivering mass death ever developed. And yet, as Election Day came near, he had been unable to defeat the Confederacy. When the war had broken out, the total number of men under arms in the United States was less than 28,000; under Lincoln's leadership, the Union Army had lost more than twenty times that number as casualties.

Those were the victor's own victims. The statistics concerning Confederate deaths have been lost, but the enormity of the losses was described some twenty years later by one of its veterans: "The day that we surrendered our Regiment, it was a pitiful sight to behold," wrote Private Sam Watkins of North Carolina. "If I remember correctly, there were just sixty-five men in all, including officers, that were paroled on that day.... a Grand Army, you may say. Three thousand, two hundred men! Only sixty-five left!"

A conservative estimate places total casualties, North and South, in excess of a million dead and mutilated human beings. A century after the Battle of Gettysburg, souvenir-hunting tourists could pick through tray after tray of minnie-balls fused together in midair collision, so heavy had been the fire.

The economists have calculated that while life under Abraham Lincoln went down in value, prices came within only a few percentage points of doubling from 1860 to 1865. According to some estimates, the total cost of the war itself was approximately $20 billion—a sum vastly in excess of the total income of the United States from its founding in 1789 until almost the beginning of World War I. And although wages increased by as much as one-third in the final year of the war, only then were they beginning to catch up with the increase in the price of staples—in the middle of the war, there was an *annual* increase of 40 percent in the cost of corn, and barley's prices had nearly doubled. Small wonder, then, that Union troops were frequently called back from the front to break strikes of unionizing workers at home.

Not that there wasn't money to be made. A select few piled up millions by dealing in illegal whiskey and contraband cotton, by speculation, and by general dishonesty sufficiently rampant to cause Ulysses S. Grant (whose myopic tendencies in such areas were dramatically evidenced during his own Presidency) to comment: "No honest man has made money in West Tennessee in the last year, while many fortunes have been made there during the time."

After four years of total and devastating war, all contemporary observers predicted an ignominious defeat for Abraham

Lincoln. They all looked back to 1860, when only Lincoln's finely honed political instincts gave him more of a mandate than his opponent, when he ran as one of three major-party candidates and gained the office only through an Electoral College majority so disproportionate to his minority share of the popular vote as to provoke the Southern movement toward separation. Then, in 1860, he had run as the nominee of the four-year-old Republican party; in his second effort, in 1864, he chose to drop the label.

After more than three years of war, the people were growing restless; they were tired of short rations at home and defeat on the battlefield; they were tired of his equivocation about slavery, despite the long-promised and only recently delivered Emancipation Proclamation; they were growing restive about the increasing tendency on the part of the administration to close opposition newspapers, and they were worried about the abrogation of the right to a writ of habeas corpus and the quiet nighttime arrests of their neighbors.

LINCOLN, a supreme politician, recognized the electorate's restiveness, so he rid himself of the Republican party and in 1864 ran as the creator and leader of the National Union party.

A classic coalition government, it was a mating of Northern Republicans with the splintered Northern factions of the Democratic party. It required the presence of the Southern Unionist Democrat who was military governor of Tennessee, Andrew Johnson, on the ticket with the Western Republican President.

And regardless of the many Republicans who have delivered no matter how many speeches to the contrary on Lincoln's birthday anniversaries, Abraham Lincoln did not take the oath of office in 1865 as a Republican. Consummate politician that he was, he had solidified a European-style parliamentary coalition of Republicans, abolitionists, and pro-Union Democrats around the National Union party in order to eke out a small margin for electoral victory. It was a party that he alone had created, and which he alone could hold together. Not only was the nation itself divided, but the North—the Union-enforcer—had no majority political party save for the unlikely combination that Abraham Lincoln alone had created and that he alone was capable of perpetuating and controlling.

WINNING THE 1865 ELECTION would make him the first American president to become more powerful than the Constitution itself. Winning that election would make him a war President elected under the aegis of a political party that was his own creation—for the first time in American history, the President would be the State; possessed of the powers which only a wartime President could have, in command of the largest army in American history, controlling his own personal national political party, he would at the same time become a classic target for political assassination. With his death, the political coalition would disperse, the command of the armies would become leaderless, and the unique wartime powers which he had nurtured for four years would be difficult for a successor to claim.

But Lincoln was a politician, not an historian. And politicians try to win elections.*

AS LINCOLN BEGAN ORGANIZING his own campaign, the Southern Democrats—known as Rebels in the North—inaugurated a unique effort.

Many months earlier, a Confederate agent named Beverly Tucker had been sent to Canada as a spy, and in that important spring of 1864 he wrote Jefferson Davis from the northern British provinces proposing that a formal commission be sent to the English colony north of the North "to create diversion and

---

* To use the word "politician" for Abraham Lincoln redefines the term. He was a man whose entire public life exemplifies a unique ability to use all his talents at manipulation in order to advance his programs, rather than himself. He was unquestionably our finest politician—but only in the highest sense of the word.

disaffection in the North and to promote war with England via Canada."

Acting upon the advice of Tucker and others, Confederate Secretary of State Judah P. Benjamin summoned a man named Jacob Thompson to Richmond. In a secret session attended only by Benjamin, Thompson and President Jefferson Davis, verbal orders were given. Neither Thompson nor Benjamin nor Davis ever divulged the subject of their conversation;* the only record of the purpose of Thompson's mission is therefore his formal commission:

April 27, 1864
Honorable Jacob Thompson, Sir:
Confiding special trust in your zeal, discretion, and patriotism, I hereby direct you to proceed at once to Canada, there to carry out such instructions as you have received from me verbally, in such manner as shall seem most likely to conduce to the furtherance of the interests of the Confederate States of America which I intrusted to you.
Very respectfully and truly yours,
Jefferson Davis

Jacob Thompson was a powerful Mississippi leader, a former U.S. senator, and, under James Buchanan, the U.S. Secretary of the Interior. Joining him were two other commissioners, Clement C. Clay, former U.S. senator from Alabama, and J. P. Holcombe, a professor of law at the University of Virginia.

Holcombe was already in Canada arranging for Confederate escapees from Northern prison camps to return to the fighting. In May 1864, Thompson arrived in Halifax, Nova Scotia, aboard the blockade-runner *Thistle*, and was followed two weeks later by Clay.

That spring they established a headquarters in the Queen's Hotel in Montreal, which at the time housed an estimated one hundred of their countrymen, and Thompson opened an ac-

---

* The nature of those orders will, however, become obvious as Mr. Thompson carries them out.

count at the Montreal branch of the Bank of Ontario with a deposit reported to be substantially more than $1,000,000.

Shortly after his arrival in Canada, Thompson made contact with Clement L. Vallandigham, an Ohio Democratic leader. A fiery peace activist, Vallandigham had been in prison during 1863 following a series of anti-Union speeches in Ohio—culminating on May 1, 1863, in Mt. Vernon, Ohio, when he declared that the war was not for the Union, but rather for the liberation of the blacks and enslavement of the whites. His imprisonment was blatantly unconstitutional, and Vallandigham made the most of it—declaring from a "military bastille" in Cincinnati on May 5, 1863: "I am a Democrat—for the Constitution, for law, for the Union, for liberty—this is my only crime."

It was an embarrassing—and nationally publicized—incident for the Lincoln administration. The President wrote General Burnside, who was responsible for the affair, that "all the Cabinet regretted the necessity of arresting . . . Vallandigham, some, perhaps, doubting that there was a real necessity," and set his mind to devising some means to get himself politically off the hook.

Lincoln's difficulty lay in the fact that there were literally thousands of Northern citizens with sympathies similar to Vallandigham. To condone such harsh treatment would be politically dangerous, but on the other hand, releasing such a Copperhead* might be interpreted as a sign of weakness that might encourage even more radical conduct. Lincoln's solution to the problem was to commute Vallandigham's sentence from imprisonment to banishment behind the Confederate lines—but the incident had created such publicity that Vallandigham was nominated for the governorship of Ohio on the Democratic ticket. Moreover, within a short time he had escaped from the South to issue lengthy polemics from his new base at Windsor,

---

* Noting that the Copperhead strikes without warning, Unionists applied the label to any who did not fully support the war.

Canada, and he finally returned to Ohio to assume a major role in the political campaign of 1864. Despite the fact that the terms of Vallandigham's banishment included provision for his reimprisonment in the event he returned to the United States, Lincoln maintained a hands-off policy. For his part, Vallandigham returned to stumping the state, while in Washington his attorneys unsuccessfully pled in February 1864 to have the Supreme Court rule that the military commission which convicted him had exceeded its jurisdiction.*

Before the war, Ohio and its sister states—Illinois and Indiana—had been centers for a brand of progressive Democratic party leaders whose political sympathies lay with the South, and whose farmer constituents had more interests in common with the agrarian South than with the Eastern industrialists who dominated the rest of the North.

But those who before the war had been called "the loyal opposition" found themselves after 1861 commonly referred to as traitors. The records of the Federal Commissary General of Prisoners alone list thirteen thousand cases of citizens imprisoned for "disloyalty," which charge could be occasioned by anything from a public speech attacking the administration to privately discouraging enlistment—and this figure does not include additional thousands arrested by the Department of the Navy and the State Department. Such repressive tactics, commingled with the principles and paranoia of these anti-Republican groups, caused many who in peacetime would have been activists in the Democratic party to join a series of secret organizations known variously as "The Knights of the Golden Circle," "The Order of American Knights," and "The Sons of Liberty." Unionist paranoia, for its part, soon inflated the membership of these groups into the hundreds of thousands,

---

* The position of the Supreme Court throughout the war had been to avoid hearing any cases which might limit the emergency powers or prerogatives of the Executive Branch. Vallandigham's case, however, along with many similar cases, would be reversed shortly after the end of the war.

and escalated their purpose from a simple desire to defeat Lincoln at the polls to the advocacy of an open and armed rebellion.

The Confederates also listened to the rumors. And when Thompson approached Clement Vallandigham, it was therefore with a desire to propose and promote the "Great Northwest Conspiracy"—an armed uprising by Southern sympathizers in the states of Indiana, Ohio and Illinois. According to the plan, these three states would declare themselves to be the "Northwest Confederacy" and would seize the U.S. arsenals within their borders in order to arm themselves and release Confederate prisoners of war who were being held in the northern sections of these states—principally, on Johnson's Island in Lake Erie.

For his part, Vallandigham turned Thompson's offer quietly aside, but the Ohio leader's rhetoric made him sound favorably disposed, particularly to a secret group within his own organization which, while sharing his opposition to Lincoln's policies, nevertheless did not share his loyalty to the Union. Allying himself with this group, Thompson was able to report to Richmond that July 20, 1864, was targeted as the date for an uprising; but soon he was writing Confederate Secretary of State Judah P. Benjamin that the date had been changed to August 16 in order to provide time in which to hold a series of meetings to prepare the public mind for an uprising. The first of these meetings was held at Peoria, Illinois. It was "a decided success," Thompson wrote Benjamin, "the vast multitudes who attended seemed to be swayed by but one leading idea—peace."*

---

* The Peoria Convention was promoted by James W. Singleton who, like Vallandigham, was denounced as a Copperhead intending to make peace with the traitors. This period can perhaps be best understood if it is compared with the era of the McCarthy outrages, the 1950's. The difference between disagreement and disloyalty becomes less clear as emotion increases. The Democrats, Vallandigham and Singleton—like Dean Acheson and George Marshall in the latter day—were loyal and earnest Americans,

Thompson, however, was misreading the peace movement in the Northwest every bit as incorrectly as Lincoln's agents were prone to do, mistaking opposition for treason. Apparently it was Thompson himself who presented Lincoln with a golden opportunity to become a peace candidate. The publisher of the New York *Tribune,* Horace Greeley, was contacted—apparently on Thompson's initiative—with the message that "two ambassadors of Davis & Co. are now in Canada, with full and complete powers for a peace," and "the whole matter (could) be consummated by me, you, them, and President Lincoln." An idealist who favored peace and incidentally opposed the Lincoln administration,* Greeley wrote President Lincoln after receipt of the message: "I venture to remind you that our bleeding, bankrupt, almost dying country also longs for peace; shudders at the prospect of fresh conscriptions, of further wholesale devastations, and of new rivers of human blood. And a wide-spread conviction that the government and its . . . supporters are not anxious for peace . . . is doing great harm."

Lincoln, moving cautiously, replied to Greeley that he was prepared to offer Jacob Thompson, Clement Clay, J. P. Holcombe or any of the other Southern "commissioners" a formal letter of safe conduct to Washington. Much to Greeley's chagrin, Lincoln also asked the *Tribune*'s editor—since the entire negotiation had become public knowledge—to serve as his own emissary to the meeting that Thompson had proposed be held at Niagara Falls.

---

compelled by honest disagreement with the policies of the majority of their countrymen to oppose those policies. The difficulty, of course, is that while Vallandigham rejected Thompson's offer, he did not in fact do anything to prevent a man whom he knew to be an agent of the Confederacy from peddling his wares to more receptive ears.

* On the night Lincoln was killed, Greeley's chief editor stopped publication of an editorial which the publisher himself had written. Confronted with his heresy the next day, the editor explained to Greeley that if he had permitted the editorial to run, the *Tribune* would have undoubtedly been burned to the ground. The text itself exists in neither of the participants' memoirs.

When Greeley reported from Niagara Falls that the Confederate representatives lacked the credentials for entering into negotiations, Lincoln seized the opportunity and placed in Greeley's hands the following: "To whom it may concern: Any proposition which embraces the restoration of peace, the integrity of the whole Union, and the abandonment of slavery, and which comes by and with an authority that can control the armies now at war against the United States, will be received and considered by the Executive Government of the United States, and will be met by liberal terms on other substantial and collateral points."

Even the editor of the *Tribune* was required to note the magnanimity of the President's offer—though it seemed magnanimous only to Unionists, and was totally objectionable to such men as Jefferson Davis. The sheer drama of a President of the United States offering to speak of peace with any representative of the opposition would soon be joined by welcome news of Union victories on the battlefield to produce for Lincoln a 400,000-vote majority on Election Day.

As the election came near, however, Lincoln took no chances.

Nevada, though not yet a state, was known to be strong for Lincoln—and just eight days before the election, after much rushing about on the part of Lincoln and his supporters, the President happily proclaimed it a State of the Union, making its electors eligible to cast their ballots. The President and his managers had been moving forcefully, if quietly, to exercise those electoral advantages to which only an incumbent President has access. All of the federal jobs at Lincoln's disposal were filled with supporters—customs men, postmasters, U.S. marshals, judges; all positions went to Lincoln's supporters or the underlings of his supporters—and the near 100 percent turnover in federal civil employment during Lincoln's administration places him in the front ranks of American spoilsmen.

Quiet midnight arrests—under Lincoln's own proclamation

suspending the right to a writ of habeas corpus*—had been utilized to quell the final plans of the creators of the Great Northwest Conspiracy to stage an uprising on Election Day. There may have been other political reasons for the arrests, as well—they kept many a Democrat away from the ballot box—but the arrests, along with the votes of furloughed Lincoln-voting soldiers and their peace-supporting civilian counterparts, served to give Lincoln the electoral votes of all three "Conspiracy" states—Illinois, Indiana and Ohio.

"All the power and influence of the War Department, then something enormous from the vast expenditure and extensive relations of the war, was employed to secure the re-election of Mr. Lincoln," wrote Assistant Secretary of War Charles A. Dana.

Jacob Thompson, however, wasn't waiting for Election Day. He had been sent to a foreign country by his own nation's Secretary of State to gain every advantage available from four years' tension between the United States and England. Along with the plots and schemes in the Northwest, Thompson would —five weeks before the election itself—begin to play his trump.

---

* There is strong evidence that Lincoln was reluctant to impose these suspensions of civil liberties. He was trying to run a democracy during a civil war—and before damning his suspensions of civil liberties, imagine what a man interested in furthering personal power might have done under such conditions. Lincoln was no tyrant—though a Southerner could amass much evidence to the contrary.

CHAPTER

III

Border Incidents

ONCE IT BECAME EVIDENT that the Union was facing civil war, the empires of Europe began acting on the assumption that internal warfare in one-third of North America meant open season on the rest of the Western Hemisphere. Spain immediately occupied Santo Domingo while France and England completed preparations and sent a joint debt-collecting force against Mexico. Civil war in the United States effectively pulled the teeth from the Monroe Doctrine, as both Lincoln and Seward knew, and all the world assumed the two leaders—if victorious over the South—would not take long to correct that situation.

Particularly vulnerable to a postwar United States attack, Canada during the Civil War was still largely an uncharted and un-unified wilderness made up of independent provinces not yet united into a nation. During the period of the U.S. Civil War, the unification movement in Canada progressed forward rapidly —and much of the motivation for unity came from the belief that the expansionists in the United States could see new states being carved from Canadian land. Lincoln's own Secretary of State—William H. Seward—had built his career espousing manifest destiny. What was even more dangerous, from the Canadian point of view, was that Seward had spent much of his time while governor of New York building a firm political base among the Irishmen—that same group whose "Fenian Brotherhood" looked to Canadian territory as an ideal location for a "new Ireland" free of the English conquerors' heel.*

Bolstering those Canadian assumptions, English diplomats knew that throughout his public career William Henry Seward had been noted for his dislike of the English, and for his belief that the United States would ultimately expand its borders to include all of Mexico and all of Canada—and for that matter, he had never retracted his often-expressed belief that in the future the "honestly obtained" dominion of the United States would unquestionably include Canada.†

Upon being named Secretary of State in 1861, Seward promptly manifested his beliefs in an official communiqué to the government of England, warning them of the consequences attached to any show of friendship to the Southern states.**

---

* For years after the Civil War, Canadians would worry about an invasion of Americanized Irishmen, and in 1867—about the time Seward bought Alaska—an abortive invasion did in fact take place. For those who appreciate the macabre in history, it should also be noted that the rim of Abraham Lincoln's coffin was, for no known reason, decorated with silver shamrocks.
† Stepping still in that direction, in 1867 he would add Alaska to the Union as "Seward's Folly," in the firm belief that it would not long be separated geographically from the rest of the states of the Union.
** One of the great men in our history, Seward began his career as Secretary of State in the Lincoln administration convinced that the President was a log-splitting dunce and all Englishmen were evil. He had, however, an ability to grow in office which is all too rare among our public men—and by the end of his term he would be one of the few to recognize Lincoln's genius. He would also be the man who worked faithfully and hard through four long years to avoid war breaking out between the Union and the British Empire.

When diplomatic recognition of the Confederacy is distinctly performed, we from that hour shall cease to be friends and become once more, as we have twice before been forced to be, enemies of Great Britain . . . a war not unlike it between the same parties occurred at the close of the last century. Europe atoned by forty years of suffering for the error that Great Britain committed in provoking that contest. If that nation shall now repeat the same great error, the social convulsions which will follow may not be so long, but they will be more general. When they shall have ceased it will, we think, be seen, whatever may have been the fortune of other nations, that it is not the United States that will have come out of them with its precious Constitution altered or its honestly obtained dominion in any degree abridged.

Distrust of Seward made it easy for many Englishmen—led by the London *Times*—to note that the Southern Confederacy had demonstrated no threat to the United States, but rather had insisted only upon a willingness to be permitted to go its own way in peace—only the desire of free men to choose both the form of their government and the personality and beliefs of the men who led it.

Emotionally and philosophically, if not politically, the desire of the South to withdraw from the Union—as America itself had done from England—failed to gain the full support of Europeans only because of the continuation of "the peculiar institution," as Seward had named it—human slavery. And Seward kicked even that supporting peg from under his own position by repeated declarations that the war was intended to preserve the Union rather than to abolish slavery.*

---

* In Seward's defense, since he had spent a good many years as an abolitionist, it must be noted that Lincoln alone was the creator of this position, in the knowledge that proclaiming general abolition would lose for the Union the border states of Kentucky, Tennessee and Western Virginia. This immoral position would create international problems for Seward with such prominent men as the Duke of Argyll, who would be required to note "that the North is not entitled to claim all the sympathy which belongs to a cause which they do not avow; and which is promoted

Border Incidents / 31

To sustain a prolonged war against an industrialized North, the agricultural South depended for its survival on an alliance with England. And so, into the political and philosophical considerations aroused by the Civil War in America, numerous Confederate emissaries were dispatched to England to discuss a hard practical matter: cotton.

Britain's navy had been born in the need of a small island for commerce—and the success of that navy at extending and protecting her avenues for importing raw materials and exporting finished goods had given Queen Victoria an empire. Among her most valuable suppliers of raw material were most of the seceding American states.

The English people had split into two camps—cotton Englishmen and abolition Englishmen—almost from the moment the first shots were exchanged at Fort Sumter. Seward's problem from the outset had been to keep the cotton Englishmen sufficiently fearful of losing Canada to mind their manners, while at the same time minding his own manners sufficiently to avoid provoking the hostility of the abolition Englishmen. Canada was the key to his foreign policy—and he danced a careful jig about it, threatening to invade when England seemed ready to come in on the Southern side, and carefully backing off from an invasion as the English mood for intervention waned.

For its part, however, Victoria's government was also playing a careful game; and while Englishmen were reluctant to risk losing Canada, they were more unwilling to relinquish their imperial prerogatives. As early as 1861 it had seemed that all the South's dreams for an alliance with England might come true when, after the British ship *Trent* had been boarded by American sailors and Confederate officials taken prisoner upon its decks, fifteen thousand English officers and men were hurriedly sent as reinforcements to the Canadian garrisons, and the British Secretary of State for War was known to have written of

---

only as an indirect consequence of a contest which (on their side at least) is waged for other objects, and on other grounds."

the United States: "We shall soon *iron the smile* out of their faces."

Sir Edward Bulwer-Lytton described the emotion many Englishmen felt during this period: "I had indulged the hope," he wrote a friend, "that your country might break up into two or perhaps more fragments. I regard the United States as a menace to the whole civilized world, if you are allowed to go on developing as you have been, undisturbed."

Seward backed down over the *"Trent* Affair" and laid the blame upon a belligerent ship's captain who had taken the Confederate officials, Mason and Slidell, from the British ship without realizing the international implications of such an act —and the hawks in Britain were further undercut when Seward added oblique apologies to his actions and ordered the Rebel agents placed upon a speeding Union vessel destined for London.

Lee—the dominant Southern commander—was finally given a setback at Antietam, thereupon putting the lie to the fabled invincibility of Southern arms. Lincoln's Emancipation Proclamation quickly followed, though it freed the tongues of English doves more than the limbs of Southern slaves.

The Emancipation Proclamation won abolition Englishmen to the Union's side. But British shipyards had been building merchantmen and warships for many long years by the time of the Civil War in America. In trade for cotton, Britannia's shipbuilding skills outfitted unarmed vessels which followed closely on the model of a sleek craft called the *Enrica*—or, more simply, the 290—while she floated in the Thames—but which left for sea trials and, instead of returning, was later seen bearing the name *Alabama,* and flying the stars and bars of the Confederacy while she sank Union merchantmen wherever she found them for three long and costly years.

Seward and the U.S. ambassador to London, Charles Adams, continued the policy of conciliation, and filed their protests and listed their claims and hinted at their threats, while suggesting all the while that England should wait a bit more before committing herself.

Then came three days in the summer of 1863—July 3, 4, and 5—and the most important place in America was an otherwise completely forgettable Pennsylvania farm town called Gettysburg.

In the South, Grant had been hanging on to a siege around Vicksburg, Mississippi. After Gettysburg, the surrender of its starving inhabitants would give Grant reason to write the President that "the Father of Waters flows once more unvexed to the sea."

The English shipbuilders had been hampered until shortly before Gettysburg and Vicksburg only by the need to issue their disclaimers and take care not to arm the Confederate ships they built while they remained in British waters. Ambassador Adams had for previous months concerned himself with a group of warships ostensibly being constructed for sale to France or Egypt. Relying on argument and persuasion, he had been provided with documentation that their true destination was for the service of Richmond, but the noise of hammers and saws at work continued. Following Gettysburg and Vicksburg, Adams—on Seward's instructions—played his trump: "It would be superfluous in me to point out to Your Lordship that this is war," he wrote—officially.

On September 9, England's Lord Russell blockaded the Thames River below the docks upon which the Confederate vessels were anchored. Shortly afterwards, England purchased the "non-warships."

In fact, Russell had given orders to sink the vessels, if necessary, rather than let them leave the Thames. Simply enough, the British leader was sufficiently sagacious to know that the Union army's victories meant that the Western Hemisphere could enforce its desires.

For two and a half years William Seward had demonstrated a brilliant comprehension of realpolitik years ahead of his age.

He had parlayed his own well-known desire for the annexation of Canada against British uncertainty of his ability to do so. Everyone knew the English could outfit twice the troops Seward could muster for Canada—but everyone also knew that Seward could put an army there twice as fast as Victoria could. It would take God knows what to win back the lost provinces, and England had no guarantee of what would be happening in Europe while she fought in North America.

Before Gettysburg, England held the initiative in the foreign affairs of the divided United States; after this battle, the question became one of whether or not Seward would go ahead and take Canada, anyway. It was a question he had been careful never to raise before the Union war machine was in full gear—afterwards, he didn't need to mention it. Afterwards, England could still win a full-tilt war with America, but she would lose part of Canada in the process.

Even then, it remained in Seward's interests to proceed with delicacy—the British plans to bombard the Eastern port cities were already written—and so long as the Confederacy fielded armies and held its own ports, England could count on a continental-based ally in any war with the Union.

Seward had gained the initiative, and now he had only to avoid the Confederate agents in Canada creating an incident from which neither side could find an egress in order to keep moving the South increasingly away from its friends in Europe.

BUT JUST AS ENGLAND HAD ITS HAWKS, so was Seward plagued by Anglophobes among both the American people and their elected officials.

Those English doves who worried about the publicly hawkish poses of the American Secretary of State would find little to be calmed by if they turned their attention to the U.S. Congress. There, Senator Charles Sumner—chairman of the Foreign Relations Committee—spoke for many of his countrymen when he explained the long-range view in a speech at Cooper Union shortly after the Battle of Gettysburg:

"I know not if a Republic like ours can count even now upon the certain friendship of any European power," Sumner noted. ". . . It will be for us to change all this and we shall do it . . . stretching from ocean to ocean—teeming with population—bountiful in resources of all kinds—and thrice-happy in universal enfranchisement—it will be more than conqueror. Nothing too vast for its power; nothing too minute for its care. . . . Strong in its own mighty stature—filled with the fulness of a new life and covered with a panoply of renown, it will confess that no dominion is of value which does not contribute to human happiness . . . and whenever any member of the Human Family is to be succored, there its voice will reach. . . . It can know no bounds to its empire over a willing world."

But if in comparison Sumner made even Seward seem to be unambitious in his expansionism, still the Foreign Relations' chairman at least made no secret of the fact that he felt winning the Civil War to have first priority: "But the first stage," Sumner said, "is the death of slavery." Following Gettysburg, everyone in the world—including the Union and England—except for Jefferson Davis, seemed to understand it was only a matter of time until that "first stage" would be reached.

Conquest by the United States had always been a subject for Canadian worry. But in the months between the Battle of Gettysburg and the fall of 1864, the Canadians grew to generally fear the Union army. The British minister to Washington, Lord Richard Lyons, was sent to Canada in the summer of 1864 to assess the military situation and reported back to London that the North could pour one-half million well-armed and well-trained troops across the border almost at will—while the combined forces of England and Canada could do little to stop them. Still another report declared without qualification that in the event of war all of Canada West would have to be surrendered, and most Englishmen and Canadians agreed with the British official who wrote: "It would be just as possible for the United States to sustain Yorkshire in a war with England, as for us to enable Canada to contend against the United States."

Queen Victoria herself wrote during this period about "America and the danger, which seems approaching, of our having a war with her, as soon as she makes peace; of the impossibility of our being able to hold Canada, but we must struggle for it...."

IN THE LATE SUMMER OF 1864, Jacob Thompson began a new phase of his operations. Confederate prisoners of war were being kept along the Great Lakes in various prisons. Thompson's new plan was to storm the prisons and free the prisoners, sending them armed and rampaging southward against the Union. He therefore instituted a hasty waterborne operation—hasty because the Great Lakes freeze sufficiently during the winter to make shipping impossible. (When the sister-in-law of the British governor-general of Canada asked him if war with the United States would come, he refused to answer, leaving her to write in her diary only that "they hope it won't come until summer is over.")

THOMPSON'S NEW PLANS began on a September evening in 1864, when several young men in civilian clothing stepped from the dock in Detroit, Michigan, onto the deck of a lake steamer called the *Philo Parsons*.

From Detroit, the *Parsons* would cross Lake Erie during the night to Canada, where she would discharge some passengers and baggage while boarding others, as she had done in small-shuttle-boat fashion for years, and make the return voyage back to the United States. This voyage, however, would break the routine.

During the overnight passage, the young travelers drew scant attention save, perhaps, for giving the appearance of paying untoward attendance to a battered and heavy old trunk several of them had carried aboard—and save for the fact that none of them disembarked at dawn on September 19 when the *Parsons* pulled into its berth at Sandwich, Canada.

There, another young man stepped aboard.

HIS NAME WAS JOHN YATES BEALL, and he held a commission as acting master in the Confederate States Navy. The twenty men aboard the *Parsons*—and, along with them, the guns carefully stored in the battered trunk—were under his direct command.

Their orders: Capture the *Parsons* and sail her against the only United States military ship in operation on the Great Lakes—the *Michigan*.

IT WAS A COMPLEX PLOT. For weeks, a Rebel spy had been ingratiating himself with the *Michigan*'s officers, hoping they would accept his offer to come aboard the night of September 19 heavily laden with supplies for a party. With luck, the painstaking weeks he'd spent earning the friendship and trust of the Union sailors would be rewarded by having their drunkenness even the odds between the *Michigan*'s heavy deck guns and the small arms Beall's men had been able to smuggle aboard the *Parsons*.

After winning the *Michigan*, the Confederates would use her to liberate the Confederate prisoners of war—many of them hardened guerrilla fighters—who were held under a light guard in a camp on Johnson's Island in Lake Erie, just off Sandusky, Ohio. Freed, the former POWs would join the *Michigan*'s now-Confederate crew in attacking federal armories in the North; then, free and armed, they would begin marching south from the lakes to trap Union armies between themselves and Lee's army of northern Virginia.

LIKE MOST OF THE PLANS laid by the Canadian Confederates, however, Beall's affair began going awry almost from its beginning. No sooner had he taken over the *Parsons* than another civilian steamer, filled with Union troops, accidentally discovered his piracy.

To their credit, the Confederates under Beall recovered from the surprise more quickly than did the Union forces, but despite his subsequent victory Beall was faced with the problem of what to do with his unwanted prisoners.

He freed them on their word to remain silent, and scuttled their vessel. Apparently his prisoners kept their pledges, but it had cost him precious time.

UNKNOWN TO BEALL, his agent aboard the *Michigan* had been unmasked hours earlier. Perhaps the delay in giving oaths to the Yankee prisoners had been his salvation—since the broad daylight forced the *Michigan's* forewarned gunners to begin firing while Beall—on the *Parsons*—still had distance enough to flee.

THE PLOT GONE AWRY, his makeshift battleship had no other choice but flight from the *Michigan's* guns. Beall hurriedly piloted it off the lake and up the Detroit River to Windsor, Canada, where he unceremoniously disembarked his men and then bored holes in her bottom to sink her.

BUT WHILE THE EXPEDITION ITSELF was an ignominious defeat, it was a decided victory when measured in terms of Confederate plans. Before the month of September was out, U.S. Secretary of State William H. Seward had been required to inform British officials that, in view of the situation on the Great Lakes, the United States would have to discontinue the Rush-Bagot Agreement, which limited the number of arms both nations could station along the joint Canada-United States border, and Union troops were dispatched to Detroit and Buffalo. For their own part, the Canadians felt compelled to send two companies of national troops to Windsor to forestall an attack from Detroit. By midfall, the border between the two countries was beginning to resemble an armed frontier, and as if to justify all the fears of the Canadians, the Rush-Bagot Agreement—though still formally in effect—was in a de facto state of suspension.

For its part, England was also preparing for the inevitable. Under special orders from Queen Victoria herself, special emissaries by the score had studied the tense situation—and all of them recommended that in the event of an attack against Canada from the United States, land troops should be withdrawn from Canadian soil while the Royal Navy attacked and destroyed all of the port cities of the north. Victoria accepted the recommendations—and issued sealed orders to commanders of the Atlantic fleet.

One of the primary newspapers in one of those port cities—*The New York Times*—was matching Victoria's militancy, declaring that the soil of Canada should be no more inviolate than the soil of Virginia: "It may be said that this will lead to a war with England. But if it must come, let it come. Not ours the guilt . . . We were never in better condition for a war with England."

BUT BEALL was only Thompson's first salvo.

On October 19, 1864—exactly a month after John Yates Beall almost began a war between England and the Union—a twenty-one-year-old senior officer of the Confederacy named Bennett Young earned a footnote in history.

"In the name of the Confederate States of America," he proclaimed from a hotel balcony in a small Vermont border town, "I take possession of St. Albans."

The Confederates would later claim Young's actions to be a reprisal for the heartless destruction which was left in Sherman's wake across South Carolina and Georgia, but within an hour the men in Young's command had taken $200,000 from the town's three banks, had murdered a civilian, and with a posse in hot pursuit, had crossed the border into Canada.

Major General John A. Dix, commander of the Military District of the East, was enjoying a dinner party in the company of England's Lord Lyons when word reached him of the St. Albans' raid.

"When the dinner had been a short time in progress," Dix would retell it later, "a telegraphic dispatch was brought to me at the table, informing me that a party of Secessionists from Canada had taken possession of the village of St. Albans in Vermont and were plundering it. Informing Mr. and Mrs. Field that I had received a communication which demanded my personal attention, I left the table, promising to return as soon as possible. I went immediately to my headquarters and telegraphed to the Commanding Officer at Burlington, the nearest military station, ordering him to send the forces at his disposal to St. Albans with the utmost despatch, and, if the marauders were still there, to capture them if possible. I instructed him also that if he came in sight of them, and they crossed the Canada line while he was in pursuit, to follow them."

THAT IS HOW EASILY an Act of War can be ordered.

"AFTER GIVING THESE ORDERS," Dix continued, "I returned to the dinner-table and, having resumed my seat, told Lord Lyons that I had been called away by a very unpleasant summons, and informed him what I had heard from St. Albans, and what orders I had given. When I added that I had ordered the marauders to be followed into Canada if our troops found it necessary he said, 'The order you have given is one of a very delicate nature, and may give us trouble.'"

Fortunately, Young's raiders had been captured by a pursuing posse of U.S. citizens and turned over to Canadian authorities before Dix's troops arrived—and even though the troops were in fact on Canadian soil, an incident was thus narrowly avoided. Even so, public opinion in the United States was aroused to such peaks over the St. Albans' incident that Seward was required to formally communicate to England that the United States was terminating the Rush-Bagot Agreement.

ON NOVEMBER 1, Acting Master John Yates Beall took command of a second Great Lakes steamer, this one purchased, rather than pirated, for $18,000 by the Confederates for the purpose of shelling the city of Buffalo. The Canadian government itself thwarted the plan this time—primarily because of a strong desire to cooperate with the Union in avoiding the war the Confederates were so busily fomenting.

Within a week, a further blow was dealt to the Canadian Confederates—Lincoln was reelected to a second term.

Assistant Secretary of War Charles A. Dana would recall years later the curious scene on election night when his President would be elected for the second time by a minority of his countrymen. "I went over to the War Department about half-past eight o'clock in the evening," Dana wrote, "and found the President and Mr. Stanton together in the Secretary's office. General Eckert, who then had charge of the Telegraph Department of the War Office, was coming in constantly with telegrams containing election returns. Mr. Stanton would read them, and the President would look at them and comment upon them."

"Have you ever read any of the writings of Petroleum V. Nasby?" Lincoln asked Dana.

Upon Dana's reply that he was only vaguely familiar with the work of the newspaper humorist, the President produced a thin yellow-covered pamphlet from his coat pocket and proceeded to read selections from Nasby's dialect columns—all of which were universally anti-Administration—aloud.

"Mr. Stanton viewed these proceedings with great impatience, as I could see," Dana noted, "but Mr. Lincoln paid no attention to that. He would read a page of a story, pause to consider a new election telegram, and then open the book again and go ahead with a new passage."

Stanton was in fact more than impatient; he was outraged. In his opinion, Nero was fiddling while Rome burned. "The idea that when the safety of the Republic was thus at issue, when the control of an empire was to be determined by a few figures brought in by the telegraph, the leader, the man most deeply concerned, not merely for himself but for his country, could turn aside to read such balderdash and to laugh at such frivolous jests was, to his mind, repugnant, even damnable," Dana wrote.

It was Lincoln's way of easing the tension, Dana would observe later—but as the returns showed more and more strongly that the President's essential pessimism had been surpassed by the supremacy of his political skills, the tension in the camp of the War Unionists eased.

Of the Union states, Lincoln carried all but Kentucky, Delaware and New Jersey. Despite large showings for McClellan in New York, Pennsylvania, Ohio, Indiana and Illinois, it had to be called a landslide.

The results brought little cheer in the camps of the Democrats and the antiwar Unionists. It brought none whatsoever to the many patrons of the Queen's Hotel in Montreal.

JACOB THOMPSON, however, had other irons in the fire.

He gave John Porterfield, a former Nashville banker, one hundred thousand dollars, with which Porterfield proceeded to New York for implementation of a financial operation which he had devised—consisting of "the purchase of gold and exporting the same, selling it for sterling Bills of Exchange, and then again converting his Exchange into gold."

The objective was to create economic crisis in the North. According to Thompson, Porterfield caused the shipment of more than two million dollars in gold at an expense of less than ten thousand dollars, and the price of gold during this period did in fact suffer inflation. Porterfield, however, found his activities cut short by the arrest of one of his former business partners.

Jacob Thompson's options were narrowing. He had begun guerrilla operations five weeks before the election. Now he would have to escalate them.

CHAPTER

IV

"Wilkes Booth Came to Washington..."

ON THE MORNING OF NOVEMBER 9, 1864, the most celebrated actor in America checked into Room 20 in the National Hotel, Washington, D.C. It had been exactly one day since the people of the Union had returned Abraham Lincoln to a second term as President of the United States.

John Wilkes Booth had spent the month of October in Montreal hobnobbing with the Confederate agents. Upon his arrival in Washington, he carried with him a letter of introduction from a Canadian-based blockade runner named Martin.*

A demented and raving and drunken maniac—that's how

---

* While in Canada, Booth had also entrusted a trunkful of priceless stage costumes to Martin. The blockade runner was subsequently captured, and the trunk along with him. Years later, it was turned over to the actor's brother Edwin, who burned the contents.

popular history would remember the brilliant and handsome young man who signed the register that day at the National Hotel. But that memory would shock his contemporaries—actors, actresses, theatre owners and stagehands alike—who considered him the finest stage talent, and warmest friend, of his day.

Earning in excess of $20,000 a year after only five years of a professional stage career, John Wilkes Booth at the age of twenty-six sacrificed a future full of wealth, fame and comfort. Of all the people involved in the assassination conspiracy, he was the only one who would certainly be recognized when he jumped from the President's box to the stage of Ford's Theatre —a theatre he had played to rave reviews numberless times. To understand why he made that sacrifice, it is first necessary to understand the man himself.

When the American theatre traces its own history back to its founding, it finds itself resting firmly on the reputation, gifts and considerable talent of Junius Brutus Booth. The most famous actor in England, the father of John Wilkes Booth emigrated to America in 1826, accompanied only by his mistress and his favorite pony.* Within half a year he became America's most famous actor as well.

Of his children, three sons eventually had careers on the stage—Junius, Jr., as an actor and theatre manager, Edwin, who would become the founder of the contemplative school of acting which prevails to this day, and John Wilkes. Junius himself named all of the children but one—Wilkes. The boy's grandfather, an immigrant English barrister, arrived in America

---

* Junius had left a wife and newborn son behind in England when he journeyed to America. In time, his mistress—a former London flower girl named Mary Ann Holmes—bore him ten children, among them John Wilkes. It is perhaps testimony to his formidable acting talents that while living openly with Mary Ann and his children in Baltimore and making many triumphant acting tours of both England and America, some twenty-five years passed before his wife discovered his infidelity and divorced him. He then married Mary Holmes.

and proudly named the grandson after his own cousin, the famed liberal English parliamentarian John Wilkes, who had led British support of the American revolution.

After the death of Junius in 1853, the older brothers—Edwin and Junius, Jr.—had gone back "on the road," following in his footsteps, and leaving young John Wilkes Booth to take care of the Maryland home that had come to be called "The Farm."

It wasn't until three years after his father's death that the kind of opportunity from which stage legends grow was presented to John Wilkes Booth. He was then seventeen years old, and through the influence of his sister's suitor, the comedian John Sleeper Clarke, he found himself playing in a performance of *Richard III*—the very play upon which his father's career had been gloriously launched under similar circumstances. The audience, however, was booing by the end of the performance.

John quietly returned to The Farm, where he resumed his duties as teen-aged head of the household with what would be remembered by everyone as good humor and warmth. He was by no means a quiet boy, but neither is there any recorded instance of insanity. Despite a tendency to go riding around at breakneck speeds and every now and again taking a shot at a neighbor's pig or cat,* he seemed to be happy and competent in his role as a farmer. He became an expert horseman, and his ability as a marksman was often demonstrated by his laying a whiskey bottle on its side, stepping back several paces, and then firing through the neck to break the bottom without harming the rest of the bottle.

---

* Incidents from this period of Booth's childhood are frequently quoted as evidence of incipient insanity. When researched fully, they become clearly little more than youth's exuberance. An example: The story is often told that during this period Booth demonstrated a tendency toward violence when he beat a neighbor with a stick. The facts are that the neighbor cursed Mother Booth and Asia, after which Booth demanded that the man apologize. When the man suggested he had no reason to apologize to such women, Booth—in the required response of a Southern man—defended the honor of his womenfolk.

He was remembered to delight that his own room at The Farm faced to the east, and proclaimed the setting sun to be "too melancholy; let me see him rise." In his room there were no rugs to muffle the woody smell of the floor, which he enjoyed, and hanging from a huge pair of antlers on the wall were swords, pistols, daggers, and a rusty old blunderbuss. Beside his schoolbooks in the bookcase were volumes of Bulwer, Byron, and Shakespeare, histories of Greece and of Rome, and small collections of Longfellow, Whittier, Milton and Poe occupying bookcase space along with collections of dried flowers, rocks and mounted insects.

"Amid his associates and with those who knew him well," wrote his niece, Blanche deBar Booth, "he was loved for his kindly nature, his generosities, and the qualities of a refined gentleman. In my early girlhood, I lived a long time with my Grandmother Booth in Baltimore. I shall always remember John, as we called him, as a very lovable boy."

Asia Booth remembered that her younger brother "was not quick at acquiring knowledge, he had to plod, progress slowly step by step, but that which he once attained he never lost. He found it far from easy to keep up with his classmates, but when the monthly review came he had not to re-study like the rest. What he had once learned remained, as he said, stamped on the side of his mind, for he not only recollected, but saw it, so as to be able to turn to the part of the page immediately. He possessed a tenacious, rather than an intuitive intelligence like his brothers. If he failed to compass a subject with such ease, at least he brought greater application and more energy to his work than they . . . in committing to memory passages of Byron's GIAOUR he was so laughably persistent in the task that the household became familiar with the passages of the poem; yet he had not forgotten a word when, years later, he was called upon to recite them, for in the interim they had lain fast locked in memory."

But if the years passed with relative comfort and happiness, still John Wilkes Booth found himself describing farming as "trying to starve respectably by torturing the barren earth"; and fully mindful of his earlier failure, in 1859 he set out once more for the stage, joining the Richmond, Virginia, stock company of George Kunkel. This time he stuck with the decision, and within two years he was a star, as well as manager of his own company in Montgomery, Alabama.

By 1863 he was being billed wherever he played with advertisements similar to one put up by Grover's Theatre in Washington: "J. Wilkes Booth, The Pride Of The American People, The Youngest Tragedian In The World, Who Is Entitled To Be Denominated A STAR OF THE FIRST MAGNITUDE...."

In the North, the Boston *Transcript* had described him in 1862 with the words: "Last evening Mr. John Wilkes Booth made his first appearance in Boston in the difficult character of RICHARD III. . . . Wilkes Booth reminds us of his father in many respects, though he does not imitate him. There are strong indications of genius in his acting and he is perhaps the most promising young actor on the American stage."

But no matter how well they had loved him in Boston, John Wilkes Booth was at least equally popular in the South, even in that sectional time*: "On the American stage the name of Booth is truly a tower of strength, an evidence of which was last night presented by the brilliant assemblage of 'brave women and men' that graced the Old Drury to welcome the youngest scion of that gifted family to those boards which had been the scene of the many and oft-repeated triumphs of his distinguished father and scarcely less distinguished brother," the New Orleans *Daily True Delta* reported in 1864. "The fame of Mr. Booth, as a young tragedian of extraordinary promise, had preceded him, and if his powerful delineation of the 'bloody-minded Gloucester' is to be taken as a sample of

---

* It should be remembered that there was a Civil War going on at the time.

his ability, then we cheerfully add our mete of admiration to the general praise and commendation his efforts have met with wherever he has appeared."

"Pictures of John Wilkes Booth," actor W. J. Ferguson commented, "in the main, disclose him as saturnine. They show little of his quick excitability and nothing of his love of fun, no trace of his joyousness. For these qualities, in common with all members of our company, I held him in admiration and high esteem. . . . Practical jokes of his invention appealed to me as the quintessence of humor. . . . If he was insane or bordering on insanity, he gave me no such idea. . . . His verve and fire as an actor made him stand high in the scale of my ideals." Drama critic William Winter remembered that "with members of the dramatic profession he was a favorite. The late Mrs. G. H. Gilbert, who acted with him, entertained a high opinion of him. McCullough liked him. So did John S. Clarke.* So did the late Edwin Varrey, a fine actor and one of the best of men. . . . Everybody was horrified at his terrible crime. . . . The stage associates of John Wilkes Booth at first utterly disbelieved and scoffed at the statement that he had shot the President . . . declaring it incredible that such a man could do such a deed."

Sir Charles Wyndham, trained in England as a surgeon, felt strongly enough about his own abolitionist beliefs to offer his services as a doctor to the Union at the onset of the Civil War. An accomplished actor as well as a doctor, he worked at Grover's Theatre when not tending wounded soldiers, and there met John Wilkes Booth. The two men struck up a warm friendship. "A marvelous man," Wyndham would later describe Booth. "He was one of the few to whom that ill-used term of genius might be applied with perfect truth. He was a genius, and a most unfortunate one. His dramatic powers were of the best. They were untutored, untrained. He lacked the quality of the student that Edwin possessed, but the artist was there.

* John S. Clarke was the husband of Asia Booth, John Wilkes Booth's sister.

"Seldom has the stage seen a more impressive, or a more handsome, or a more impassioned actor. Picture to yourself Adonis, with high forehead, aesthetic face corrected by rather full lips, sweeping black hair, a figure of perfect youthful proportions and the most wonderful black eyes in the world. Such was John Wilkes Booth.

"At all times his eyes were his striking features, but when his emotions were aroused they were like living jewels. Flames shot from them. His only physical defect was his height (for certain heroic characters) . . . but he made up for the lack by his extraordinary presence and magnetism. . . .

"The courtesy and kindness shown me by John Wilkes made way for friendship between us, and we were frequently together after the play. He was a most charming fellow off the stage as well as on, a man of flashing wit and magnetic manner. He was one of the best raconteurs to whom I ever listened. As he talked he threw himself into his words, brilliant, ready, enthusiastic. He could hold a group spellbound by the hour at the force and fire and beauty of him. He was unusually fluent. . . . He was the idol of women. They would rave of him, his voice, his hair, his eyes. Small wonder, for he was fascinating."

One of the women Wyndham referred to was an actress, Clara Morris, who would remember seeing John Booth seated in his dressing room at a theater dutifully clipping the names from mash letters written by female admirers before reading them. One day John Wilkes Booth caught her watching him in this endeavor and calmly announced: "They are harmless now, little one; their sting lies in the tail."

Miss Morris would remember that "his head and throat, and the manner of its rising from his shoulders, were very beautiful. His colouring was unusual; the ivory pallor of his skin, the inky blackness of his densely thick hair, the heavy lids of his glowing eyes were all oriental, and they gave a touch of mystery to his face when it fell into gravity; but there was generally a flash of white teeth behind his silky moustache and a laugh in his eyes."

Exhibiting a weak spot for him herself, Miss Morris noted that women were "mad about him."

Though he may have been discreet about his letters, John Wilkes Booth hardly lived a celibate's life. The pictures of five women were found in his wallet when he died, and a sixth attempted suicide when she heard of his death. Under his tousled forelock he carried a knife-slash scar received from a jealous paramour who also tried the knife—with an equal lack of success—upon herself. There are hints of at least one run-in with an irate husband, and during the last months of his life John Wilkes Booth enjoyed at least the companionship of an Ella in Washington, an Etta in New York, a Jennie in Canada, and an unknown young woman with whom he dallied in Boston.

But such temptations are, after all, not unusual for a young man who in current parlance would easily be rated as a superstar. Of the four biggest names in the American theatre during this period, three ended with the name Booth—Junius, even though he was dead, and his sons Edwin and John. The fourth was Edwin Forrest, who would become the first to charge John with madness. The aging last of the great melodramatic and bombastic actors of the Junius Booth school, Forrest seemed to find a Booth playing—usually to better reviews—at a competitive theatre almost everywhere he chose to perform. Usually, reviewers would note Forrest's skill and talent, but from there the review would go on to conclude either that Edwin's more deliberative interpretations were superior or that John's youth gave him an edge. The theater itself was changing—and as John took the leadership mantle from Forrest in the activist school, Edwin was founding a totally new style of acting that would in a decade find him revered even beyond his father.

But Edwin's dominance was in the future. By 1863—at only twenty-four years of age—John Wilkes Booth had come to be ranked among the titans of the American theater. His fame and fortune were only a part of it—and to his $20,000 annual return from the stage can be added additional monies from his reputed financial interests in the oil fields of Pennsylvania and Canada. In many ways, he was the first of America's matinee idols, and his mass-produced portraits adorned the dressers of countless young women who considered him the most handsome man in America. Billed at Ford's Theatre in that year as "the young and distinguished tragedian," he had even been given the honor of playing the lead role in a contemporary hit called *The Marble Heart*, during one of the rare occasions upon which the U.S. President Abraham Lincoln had been able to steal a few hours' respite from civil war.*

ON NOVEMBER 9, when he checked into the National Hotel, John Wilkes Booth had a brilliant future before him. Two days later he began a course which would destroy that future.

He left no personal memoirs directly explaining why. He had apparently spent some time the previous summer both in Canada and in Washington. The previous spring he had, for unknown reasons, begun to refuse theatre bookings. On October 27, 1865, he had deposited two hundred dollars in cash and a check from a broker named Davis in a Montreal bank, and bought a bill of exchange for slightly more than sixty-one pounds.

The evidence concerning how John Wilkes Booth moved from American Idol to Contemporary Judas is scanty. Perhaps that is why historians have been so tempted to go along with the delusion of his insanity.

On November 11, Wilkes left the National and then Wash-

* John Wilkes Booth had been booked at Ford's for a two-week engagement during which "all of the celebrated Shakespearean Tragedies would be produced." It was a slight overstatement, but Washington audiences were as partial to enjoying Booth as audiences everywhere else were, and during this tour they could watch him in ample variety: *Richard III, The Merchant of Venice, Hamlet, Romeo and Juliet,* and four popular melodramas of *The Marble Heart* variety. It is well to note that the scheduled performances were the most rigorous ever undertaken by a performer at Ford's—involving eight separate plays to be performed on twelve of thirteen straight nights. The *National Intelligencer*'s reviewer called Booth's Romeo "the most satisfactory of all renderings of that fine character."

ington, crossing the Anacostia River over the bridge he would later take for his escape, and traveled deep into the Maryland Peninsula. "He brought a letter of introduction to Dr. Queen from someone in Montreal of the name of Martin, I think," an eyewitness* remembered, stating that "this man Booth wanted to see the county. Booth's object in visiting the county was to purchase lands; he told me so himself, and made various inquiries of me respecting the price of land there, and about the roads in Charles County. I told him that land varied in price from five to fifty dollars per acre; poor land being worth only about five dollars, and land with improvements or on a river would be worth fifty dollars; but I could not give him much information with regard to these matters, and referred him to Henry Mudd, Dr. Mudd's father, a large landowner. . . . On the next morning, Sunday, I accompanied him and Dr. Queen to church at Bryantown. I happened to see Dr. Samuel A. Mudd in front of the church before entering, and spoke to him, and introduced Mr. Booth to him."

Wilkes returned to the National Hotel on the evening of November 14, leaving it on November 16 to join his brother Junius, Jr., in Baltimore. Shortly thereafter, the two distinguished brothers traveled together to New York City for what many people believed would be the most significant theatrical event of the decade.

Edwin Booth had dreamed for quite some time about staging Shakespeare's *Julius Caesar* with himself, Junius and Wilkes in the leading roles—and he had selected November 25 as the date upon which the three would "do honor to the immortal Bard from whose works the genius of their father caught its inspiration, and of many of whose greatest creations he was the best and noblest illustrator the stage has ever seen." The profits

---

* Dr. Queen's son-in-law, John C. Thompson. It should be remembered that Martin is the name of the blockade runner Booth met among the Confederate agents in Montreal, and the man to whom he entrusted the care of his expensive theatrical costumes.

from the single performance were to be given over to erect a statue to Shakespeare in New York's Central Park.*

More than two thousand people crowded the Winter Garden that night to watch Junius as Cassius, Edwin as Brutus, and Wilkes as Mark Antony, and in a private box the mother of them all joined the deafening ovation as the three brothers entered side by side in the first act.

The applause and cries of "Bravo! Bravo!" were drowning out all other sounds when Act I ended, and were silenced only for a moment when all three sons walked to stand beneath Mary Booth and bow in unison, applauding in silence both her and their father.

The *New York Herald* reviewed the event: "Brutus was individualized with great force and distinctness—Cassius was brought out equally well—and if there was less of real personality given to Mark Antony, the fault was rather in the part than in the actor." Thus did John Wilkes Booth, as Mark Antony, find himself in the unique position of being praised by a critic for bailing out the weak characterization of William Shakespeare.

BUT the *Herald* carried a more important story than the review: New York City had narrowly averted disaster during the night as scores of incendiary fires were ignited by Confederate terrorists operating from Canada.

"ATTEMPT TO BURN THE CITY," headlined the newspaper, reporting a "Discovery of a vast rebel conspiracy—twelve hotels fired by turpentine and phosphorus." The hotels included the famed Astor House, the Belmont, and the immense Metropolitan. The United States Hotel at Broadway and Maiden Lane was gutted, and the Bancroft on 12th Street. Ships berthed at the Hudson River docks were set afire. Panicking crowds had nearly wrecked P. T. Barnum's Museum.

---

* The statue still stands.

"Wilkes Booth Came to Washington . . ." / 55

A report to the Confederate government describing the incendiary plot against New York was signed by the leading Confederate in Canada, Jacob Thompson, and was endorsed by Judah Benjamin.

A Union double agent named Richard Montgomery later swore to being the tipster whose warning had prevented New York from burning to the ground. He also swore that John Wilkes Booth had been seen in Canada after the incendiary attack, in December. It is a significant piece of testimony, even though any statement by Montgomery—as a double agent—must be accepted with a grain of salt. Following the incendiary attack on New York City the night of November 25, there is no record of Wilkes' activities until he checked into the National Hotel again on December 12.

IN MIDWINTER 1864, Louis J. Weichmann took up residence in the boardinghouse run by Mrs. Mary E. Surratt at 541 H Street, NW, between 6th and 7th, in Washington. Five years before, Lou Weichmann and Mrs. Surratt's young son John had studied for the priesthood together at St. Charles College in Maryland. It was perhaps natural for them to renew their friendship by living under the same roof after Weichmann moved to Washington.*

On some unknown date later remembered as being only

---

* Perhaps. But the boardinghouse on H Street, like many similar homes in Washington during the Civil War, was located in the capital city only geographically. Occupants of it before Lincoln won reelection and Southern military fortunes began to wane were able to disguise their feelings—but toward the end of the war the tone of life within the boardinghouse, as elsewhere, changed abruptly and became actively Confederate. It is necessary, therefore, to note that Weichmann's position—which he took on January 9, 1864—as a clerk in the office of the Commissary-General of Prisoners gave him access to information concerning the numbers of prisoners located in various Northern prison camps, and the dates of their arrivals as well as the identification of their regiments. He was therefore a potentially very useful source of information to the Confederates in Canada, who throughout this period were bent upon carrying out various schemes to free those Confederate POWs, arm them, and send them attacking Union armies from behind the northern lines.

around Christmastime 1864, new Washington resident Weichmann was passing down 7th Street in company with John H. Surratt. When they were opposite Odd Fellow's Hall someone called, "Surratt, Surratt." Both young men turned around, and Surratt recognized "an old acquaintance of his," Dr. Samuel A. Mudd. Mudd and Surratt exchanged greetings, and then Surratt introduced Dr. Mudd to young Lou Weichmann. For his part, the doctor introduced both young men to his own companion, the famous actor, John Wilkes Booth.

"Booth invited us to his room at the National Hotel," Weichmann remembered. "When we arrived there, he told us to be seated and ordered cigars and wines for four. Dr. Mudd then went out to a passage and called Booth out, and had a private conversation with him. When they returned, Booth called Surratt and all three went out together and had a private conversation, leaving me alone. I did not hear the conversation; I was seated on a lounge near the window. On returning to the room the last time, Dr. Mudd apologized to me for his private conversations, and stated that Booth and he had some private business; that Booth wished to purchase his farm, but that he did not care about selling it as Booth was not willing to give him enough. Booth also apologized, and stated to me that he wished to purchase Dr. Mudd's farm. Afterward they were seated round the center table when Booth took out an envelope, and on the back of it made marks with a pencil. I should not consider it writing, but from the motion of the pencil it was more like roads or lines."

Weichmann did not recall seeing Booth at the Surratt home prior to this meeting, which may well have been true since the actor had been in Washington only a total of seven days since his own first meeting with Mudd at the instigation of the rebel blockade runner, Martin. However, "after this interview at the National Hotel," Weichmann recalled, "Booth called at Mrs. Surratt's frequently, generally asking for Mr. John H. Surratt, and in his absence for Mrs. Surratt. Their interviews were al-

"Wilkes Booth Came to Washington..." / 57

ways apart from other persons. I've been in the parlor in company with Booth, when Booth has taken Surratt upstairs to engage in private conversation. Sometimes, when engaged in general conversation, Booth would say, 'John, can you go upstairs and spare me a word?' They would then go upstairs and engage in private conversations which would sometimes last two or three hours. The same thing would sometimes occur with Mrs. Surratt."

CONSIDER THE CAST of characters so far introduced. Following his own sojourn with the Confederates in Canada, John Wilkes Booth has been introduced by them to Dr. Mudd. In turn, Dr. Mudd has introduced the young actor into the Surratt boardinghouse—which will come to notoriety for housing Confederate spies identified only as a Mr. Howell and a Mrs. Slater, and which includes under its roof young John H. Surratt—who has become a principal secret courier between the Confederate cabal in Canada and the office of the Secretary of State of the Confederate States of America in Richmond, Judah P. Benjamin, the very man whose initiative established the Confederate operations in Montreal and Toronto.

Of those captured and/or put on trial for the murder of President Lincoln, only three—Sam Arnold, Ed Spangler, and Mike O'Laughlin—are known to have been brought into any plot *directly* by John Wilkes Booth. Arnold and O'Laughlin were old school chums of the actor. Spangler was the carpenter who had helped Booth's father build the family home in Maryland, and who happened to be working at Ford's Theatre in the spring of 1865. *None* of these three men were sent to the gallows by the blatantly hanging judges assembled to mete out drumhead justice after Lincoln's death; *none* are recorded as being privy to any conversations concerning an assassination plot, and the bulk of the evidence indicates that *none* were in fact involved in the plot.

Booth had, however, become involved in late 1864 in the

active Confederate spy network reaching from Montreal to Richmond. Mudd had introduced him to the Surratts. The Surratts in turn will introduce him to:

David E. Herold, who will be captured with Booth at Garrett's farm: "I met the prisoner, David E. Herold," Louis Weichmann testified, "at Mrs. Surratt's on one occasion; I also met him when we visited the theater when Booth played *Pescara*; and I met him at Mrs. Surratt's in the country the spring of 1863, when I first made Mrs. Surratt's acquaintance. I met him again in the summer of 1864 at Piscataway Church. These are the only times, to my recollection, I ever met him."

George Atzerodt, who will hang: "I recognize the prisoner, Atzerodt," Weichmann testified. "He first came to Mrs. Surratt's house, as near as I can remember, about three weeks after I formed the acquaintance of Booth, and inquired for John H. Surratt, or Mrs. Surratt, as he said. Since then he must have been at the house ten or fifteen times. The young ladies of the house, not comprehending the name that he gave, and understanding that he came from Port Tobacco in the lower portion of Maryland, gave him the nickname of 'Port Tobacco.' "*

Lewis Powell, who will attack Secretary of State William Seward, on the night of April 14, 1865: "Sometime in March last, I think," Weichmann testified, "a man calling himself Wood came to Mrs. Surratt's and inquired for John H. Surratt.

---

* George Atzerodt was hanged in the belief that he had accepted an assignment to kill Vice-President Andrew Johnson on the night of April 14, 1865. Atzerodt was, however, the operator of a clandestine ferryboat carrying Confederate spies from Port Tobacco, Maryland, to the Virginia shore on the other side of Chesapeake Bay. It is unquestionably true that on the assassination night George Atzerodt was registered in the hotel room directly above that of Vice-President Johnson. It is also unquestionably true that if John Wilkes Booth had intended to escape down the Maryland Peninsula, and from there into Virginia, he would have been far more wise to have relied on Atzerodt manning his ferryboat from Port Tobacco— rather than assigning Johnson to him. However, if Booth planned instead to go north, Atzerodt would have become the most dispensable of the plotters.

I went to the door and told him Mr. Surratt was not at home; he thereupon expressed a desire to see Mrs. Surratt, and I introduced him, having first asked his name. That is the man [and at this, Weichmann pointed to Powell sitting in the prisoner's box]; he stopped at the house all night. He had supper served up to him in my room; I took it to him from the kitchen. He brought no baggage; he had a black overcoat on, a black dress coat, and grey pants. He remained 'til the next morning, leaving by the earliest train for Baltimore. About three weeks afterward he called again, and I again went to the door. I had forgotten his name, and asking him, he gave the name of Payne. I ushered him into the parlor, where were Mrs. Surratt, Miss Surratt, and Miss Honora Fitzpatrick. He remained three days that time. He represented himself as a Baptist preacher, and said that he had been in prison in Baltimore for about a week; that he had taken the oath of allegiance, and was now going to become a good and loyal citizen."*

CONSIDER AGAIN THE CAST of characters. On the night of April 14, 1865, John Wilkes Booth shot and killed Abraham Lincoln. At the same time, Lewis Powell—whom he met at the Surratt Home—attacked and attempted to assassinate the Secretary of State, William H. Seward. Accompanying Powell was David Herold, who first met Booth at the Surratt home and who was next seen in the company of Booth at a tavern owned

---

* There is a differing version which appears from time to time in narratives, in which Powell accidentally runs into Booth in Baltimore in 1864 and the two men renew a friendship that began years earlier while Booth was playing at a theater in Richmond. Weichmann's account, however, is more in keeping with the facts. After serving in both the regular Confederate Army and in guerrilla units—and after being wounded in action at Gettysburg— Powell dropped out of sight until reemerging at the Surratt home. Various accounts place him, at differing times late in the war, in both Baltimore and in Canada—and a guerrilla named Powell is listed in Canadian court records as being among a group of Confederate raiders operating against the United States from Canadian soil.

by Mrs. Surratt in Maryland. From that tavern John Wilkes Booth and David Herold immediately traveled to the home of Dr. Samuel A. Mudd—who had introduced Booth to the Surratts—in order to have Booth's broken leg treated.

These are the primary conspirators—all share only one thing in common: they are united by their contacts with the Confederate cabal in Canada.

CHAPTER V

A Small Company of Irregulars

"I KNOW I AM IN DANGER," the President once told Secretary of State Seward, "but I am not going to worry over threats like these."

Charles A. Dana found the threats—more than eighty of them—while searching Lincoln's private desk the morning after the assassination. They were gathered together in a small envelope identified, in the President's own handwriting, with the word "Assassination."

Senator Cornelius Cole remembered the President telling him that "he would not be dying all the while" after one such threat, and despite all of Secretary of War Edwin Stanton's exertions and arguments to the contrary, Lincoln spent most of the war evading the guards which the man he laughingly called "my Mars" had ordered to surround and follow him.

"Don't come out in this storm with me, boys," Lincoln remarked to some of his personal guards on one evening early in 1865 while waving them aside. "I have an umbrella and can get home safely without you."

One soldier spoke up quickly: "But, Mr. President, we have positive orders from Mr. Stanton not to allow you to return alone. You know we dare not disobey his orders."

It was a vicious night, and the distance Lincoln had to travel was less than a hundred yards from the War Department offices to the White House. But he sighed in acquiescence. "No, I suppose not. If Stanton should learn that you had let me return alone, he would have you court-martialed and shot inside of twenty-four hours."

It was not a new conflict between the two. Four years earlier, at the outset of the war, Stanton had ordered mounted guards to be posted at the carriage entrances to the White House, and others at the foot-gates, and they had been removed only after Lincoln himself had protested that they smacked more of an imperialist than a democratic government.

Despite the pressures from his friends and subordinates, Lincoln continued to follow his own course and to dream of death while eluding his guards. Lamon finally blew his stack over the latter, and at Christmastime in 1864 wrote a long threat to resign as marshal of the District of Columbia unless the President mended his ways and came to understand that, "you know, or ought to know, that your life is sought after and will be taken, unless you and your friends are cautious." Lamon would later record that the President "thought me insane upon the subject of his safety."*

"I think the Lord in his own good time and way will work

---

* Joking that Lamon was so strong he "could bend pokers over his arm," Lincoln asked the burly military officer to accompany him and Mrs. Lincoln to the theater on the night of April 14, 1865. In what may well have been an attempt by Secretary Stanton and him to dissuade the President from exposing himself to unnecessary danger, Lamon pleaded pressing duty and refused the invitation.

A Small Company of Irregulars / 63

this out all right," Lamon remembered Lincoln saying. "God knows what is best."

The President understood both the dangers and the requirements of his office. A physically powerful man, he could face the former; a politician, he had to face the latter. And so he went without guards to do his own banking and his own shopping.* And sometimes, when he could duck the guards, he went to the theater. One of those instances was when Mary Todd Lincoln was away.† Lincoln had gone alone to Ford's Theatre to watch John Wilkes Booth play in *The Marble Heart*.

Wilkes would soon—to the mystery of his fans—drop away from the stage, in the early summer of 1864. Around that time, he gave his sister Asia a sealed envelope which contained a statement of his feelings: "People of the North," Booth cries out in it, "to hate tyranny, to love liberty and justice, to strike at wrong and oppression, was the teaching of our fathers." And so it was. "The study of our early history will not let me forget it, and may it never."

He then discusses the question of slavery, pointing up an argument many espoused for twenty years before the war and a century after it: "I, for one, have ever considered *it* one of the greatest blessings (both for themselves and us) that God ever bestowed upon a favored nation. Witness heretofore our wealth and power; witness their elevation and enlightenment above their race elsewhere. I have lived among it most of my life, and have seen *less* harsh treatment from master to man than I have beheld in the North from father to son. Yet Heaven knows, *no one* would be more willing to do *more* for the negro race than I, could I but see a way to *still better their* condition." If in the concluding decades of the twentieth century mankind has risen sufficiently to reject any defense of human slavery as invalid per

---

* Numerous current Washington businesses—from optometrists to bankers —today exhibit Lincoln's personal checks to their firms.
† Mrs. Lincoln was secretly in the South, calming her sister upon the latter's unexpected widowhood, her Confederate general husband having been killed in battle.

se, still Wilkes has the right to be judged only by his peers. And few of them would disagree with his statement. Lincoln, for example, answered Southerner Alex Stephens at Hampton Roads by saying, "Let 'em root," when Stephens asked how the black people who were too old to work would be cared for after emancipation.* "But Lincoln's policy," Wilkes wrote, "is only preparing the way for their total annihilation."

Wilkes defends slavery, but recognizing that others may differ with that defense, he poses the question of whether or not the founding fathers envisioned their creation as indissoluble. Their own Declaration of Independence, Booth notes, defended their own rebellion as one forced upon them after all entreaties for a compromise were rejected.

"When I aided in the capture and execution of John Brown† (who was a murderer on our western border, and who was fairly *tried and convicted*, before an impartial judge and jury, of treason, and who, by the way, has since been made a god), I was proud of my little share in the transaction, for I deemed it my duty, and that I was helping our common country to perform an act of justice. But what was a crime in poor John Brown is now considered (by themselves) as the greatest and only virtue of the whole Republican Party. Strange transmigration! *Vice* to become a *virtue* simply because *more* indulge in it!"

Booth is taking a very Southern view here. Brown was

---

* Lincoln's comments here are from the recollections of Confederate Vice President Alexander Stephens, an old friend of Lincoln's before the war. The quote is not meant to libel the President—faced with a continuing war, pushed by the Black Republicans, what other answer could Lincoln give to such a question? It was not an issue among his priorities. Nor could it be until the war was over and the slaves were freed—neither of which had happened at the time when the quoted conversation occurred.

† There are no records of why he did it, but John Booth briefly left the stage before the war to serve under U.S. Army Colonel Robert E. Lee at the hanging of John Brown. Martyred after he mounted the scaffold, Brown had engaged in myriad bloody murders before he tried to foment a slave insurrection in what is now West Virginia, and captured for a while the U.S. arsenal there.

hanged for attacking a U.S arsenal—which is what the South did to Fort Sumter. Booth means, however, to draw an analogy with Brown's ultimate objective, which was to foment a slave rebellion. Lincoln, remember, was consistent in wanting only to save the Union, from Brown or the South.

"I have also studied hard to discover upon what grounds the right of a State to secede has been denied," Booth continues, "when our very name, United States, and the Declaration of Independence, *both* provide for secession." Booth is right on both points. Regarding his first point, most historians are in agreement that the Civil War changed phraseology from "the United States *are*" to "the United States *is*." Regarding the second point, it must be remembered that the Declaration of Independence was written by rebels, and remains to this day a justification of the very concept of rebellion. It is by definition an advocacy of secession—whether of colonies from a mother country or states from a Union. A staunch Unionist would take note that the Preamble to the Constitution begins, "We, the people of the United States . . ." and would insist that the document was therefore written by the people rather than by the several states. A secessionist such as Booth, however, could —with equal validity—move from the Constitution back to the Declaration and declare, with Jefferson, that a government is valid only when it represents everyone.

"How I have loved the *old flag* can never now be known," Booth writes. "A few years since, and the entire world could boast of none so pure and spotless. . . . But no, day by day has she been dragged deeper and deeper into cruelty and oppression, till now (in my eyes) her once bright red stripes look like *bloody gashes* on the face of heaven."*

How does a man move from fame and fortune to ignominy? How does sacrifice predominate over success? There is no need or desire here to make a martyr of a basically foolish young

---

* The italics are Booth's.

man, trained to the theater's skills and demands but as naïve as he was passionate about politics. The same could describe some signers of the Declaration of Independence.

Something happened to John Wilkes Booth after the spring of 1864. Actually, much had happened, and all of it is lost to the records.

This much is known. He had played to rave reviews and stunned audiences, both North and South, from 1859 to 1864. He had spoken openly of an empathy for the cause of self-determination—and in 1861 that meant the Confederacy. Named for a radical, he was still young enough to avoid considering the impact of his actions—and such is the difference between radicalism and liberalism or libertarianism.

Therefore, he became involved in a conspiracy of similarly young men called upon by their times to interact with a civil war. At various times, he is known to have used his fame as an actor to smuggle quinine from North to South, utilizing a "nonbelligerent" profession to carry the sadly needed drug to disease-infected soldiers of the Confederacy.

At some point, a plot arose among himself and his friends to kidnap the President of the United States. It was not so strange or ludicrous a plot as in hindsight it appears to be. A group of ministers approached Union War Secretary Stanton at about the same time with a similar plot directed at Jefferson Davis, and it was given sufficient credence that an agent was dispatched to Richmond in order to check its feasibility before it was rejected. If the U.S. government could consider such a plan not worthy of rejection out of hand, how then are we to dismiss the similar scheme of young patriots?

The story of their plot is a tangled web of lies, intrigue and counterintrigue which became only partially visible in the investigations following President Lincoln's death. What little can be known is best intuited by trying, in the mind's eye, to join them as they wait for their prey.

A Small Company of Irregulars / 67

SOUTH OF THEM, in Virginia, an army reduced to ranks of old men and very small boys was being strangled by Grant's relentless military machine; modern warfare was being discovered—the uselessness of human valor striking helplessly against metallic monsters was being demonstrated by a South now grown desperate at its own emasculation.

South of them, only one hundred miles into Virginia, there is shooting to be heard; but they hoped for no shooting on this road to the President's favorite retreat, the Soldier's Home. Lincoln had visited it frequently as a respite from Washington's heat and pressure and stink, and word had come to them that he would journey to it tonight.

To the south of them, old men and young boys were fighting to defend their right to choose their own government to follow, and to the north of them were thousands of battle-seasoned and fire-tested Southern troops being held as prisoners of war. The POWs were more closely guarded than the President in his capital. It was as simple as that.

Perhaps they crouched behind trees on either side of the road for the hours they waited, their hands upon the horses' noses to discourage sound. Perhaps, boldly, they sat upon their saddles side by side, all of them with their backs to the Soldier's Home and all their senses aimed toward Washington. This small company of irregulars—call them the Keystone Kops in hindsight, perhaps—waited this night for their prey and fancied themselves to be guerrillas.

Elsewhere, guerrilla warfare was working for The Cause. In Missouri and Kansas, Quantrill won few votes for valor, but he did sack Lawrence and he did keep Yankee troops busy outside the South. Mosby was striking successfully in the Virginia valley, and Morgan's Raiders had drawn every man in Ohio who owned a gun to the defense of Cincinnati on the mere rumor that they were heading toward it. The only real success from

Canada was Bennett Young's raid on St. Albans—and it took a lot of Seward's time to smooth it over after General Dix sent Union troops into Canada behind Young's escaping guerrillas.

Grant had the troops, the big guns and the uniforms. The South had little remaining to it. Grant lost troops and guns and clothing and mules and horses to the Confederacy, but somehow his government kept finding more of them, and he kept advancing.

Lee was losing. His trained troops had only succeeded in their goal of invading the North by joining marching columns as prisoners of war. For a while, Lincoln had insisted on continuing a program of exchanging prisoners of war with the South, but in time Grant's and Stanton's arguments had won out, and Lincoln—understanding that Lee needed his trained officers and men desperately, while the Union could replace its lost loved ones—at long last had stopped the trades.

It was therefore a natural plot. It may well have been hatched in the minds of many men at the same time: kidnap Lincoln, take him to Richmond, and then trade him for all the prisoners of war.

Wherever it was hatched, it was now to be carried out in the winter of 1864 on a lonely road between Washington and the Soldier's Home. For hours George Atzerodt had stood by his little ferryboat at Port Tobacco, indiscreetly turning customers aside by explaining that he had important business coming. Between Atzerodt at the southern tip of the Maryland Peninsula and his friends upon the roadway Sam Arnold and Mike O'Laughlin were waiting, prepared to haul taut the thick ropes stretched at hoof level between trees bordering the roadway, to trip pursuers' horses.

For hours, the collective ears of Lew Powell, John Surratt, and Wilkes Booth had listened down the road from the Soldier's Home to Washington, and only minutes after the kidnappers first heard the faint clacketing of the horses, they saw the presidential carriage coming into view around a bend. Tense minutes passed, and then at last the men made their move.

Three entire months had been spent by them in the planning and the plotting of this night, months spent in consulting maps and spent in testing disguises. "Booth took out an envelope, and on the back of it made marks with a pencil," Weichmann testified. "I should not consider it writing, but from the motion of the pencil it was more like roads or lines."

"The only evidence of disguise or preparation for it that I know of was a false moustache which I found on the table in my room one day," Weichmann noted elsewhere in his testimony. "I put the moustache into a little toilet box that was on my table. Payne afterward searched round the table and inquired for his moustache. I was sitting on a chair and did not say anything. I retained the moustache, and it was found in my baggage that was seized. On returning from my office one day while Payne was there, I went upstairs to the third story and found Surratt and Payne seated on a bed, playing with bowie-knives. There were also two revolvers and four sets of new spurs."

As an actor, Wilkes was a master of make-up. As a spy, Surratt had learned to disguise himself. As a guest in Mrs. Surratt's boardinghouse—under the names of Wood and Payne—Powell had for weeks maintained the ruse of being an itinerant preacher. The route had been planned in the boardinghouse, and along it now the other conspirators were waiting to mislead and to delay any pursuers.

In the Northern prisons, all of the captured and battle-hardened veterans of Nashville and of Gettysburg would be the reward for the success of these conspirators—all of Mosby's captured troopers, and all of the men taken in the Shenandoah Valley, and those who were with Jackson before he was killed, and those who were captured in the bloody confusion of Antietam and the fiery holocaust at the Wilderness.

So it was that John Wilkes Booth, John Surratt and Lew Powell set themselves up to overpower the sinewed politician from Illinois and take him to the South. All of Washington knew that Lincoln had been ill, and that fact, coupled with Powell's strength, might have made it an even fight—although the legends from the prairie suggested that the President was capable of damaging a physical enemy, no matter his fifty-five years of age or his month-long stomach upset. Powell stood nearly as tall as Lincoln and was half his age, and the brains of Booth and Surratt could take their two "drunk" friends at least as far as Atzerodt's ferryboat. After that journey, it would take all of Grant's army to free the President—or it would take a deal with Jefferson Davis to free the prisoners of war.

Now everything is ready as the single horse pulling the small buggy comes closer and closer to them. There are no guards. The conspirators ceremonially pull their pistols and spur their horses forward, crashing over the few yards of dirt roadway and dashing to surround the man and his carriage and his horse.

But the man is clean-shaven.

Inside the carriage, Supreme Court Chief Justice Salmon P. Chase cannot at first comprehend the commotion. He had been enjoying the leisurely ride to the Soldier's Home, by happenstance going there in Lincoln's place—and at first he cannot grasp the commotion of horsemen about the carriage, brandishing pistols reflecting the moonlight. They spew about him, their voices victorious at the beginning, each in his turn peering inside the carriage at the confused Chief Justice of the United States, and then all of them together turn and ride away, swearing at Chase and at each other, and at Bad Fortune.

They rode back to Washington at a gallop, and when they stalked back into Mrs. Surratt's boardinghouse, hot and late and angry, Louis Weichmann heard them slapping at their boots in disgust and frustration, and listened to them whispering in Powell's room as they stayed up very late and drank too much.

Perhaps they did not know it then, but after Chase told Stanton of the episode even Lincoln had to begin acquiescing to the War Secretary's demands that guards surround him. From this point on, kidnapping would be far more difficult than murder.

CHAPTER

VI

The Last Days of the Lost Cause

WAR RARELY PAUSES FOR HOLIDAYS. And so it was that, following the close of a regular business day, Good Friday 1865, Charles A. Dana turned the knob and entered the President's office in the White House. Taking a quick glance around the room and seeing no one, Dana assumed that the President had gone to his private rooms to dress for the theater, but as he turned to leave, Lincoln's voice halted him.

"Halloo, Dana!" The President called from a small side room where he stood washing his hands. "What is it? What's up?"

A former newspaperman, Dana had served throughout most of Lincoln's administration as Assistant Secretary of War, in which capacity he had visited virtually every battlefield as the eyes and ears of the government. One of his duties was to receive the reports of the various secret service operatives throughout the country, and on that afternoon of April 14 he had gotten a telegram from the provost marshal in Portland, Maine.

"I have positive information that Jacob Thompson will pass through Portland tonight," it read, "in order to take a steamer for England. What are your orders?" Dana read the telegram to the President, and when he was finished Lincoln asked if Secretary of War Stanton had made any recommendation about it.

"He says arrest him," Dana replied, "but that I should refer the question to you."

Lincoln had stepped from the privy, drying his hands upon a towel as Dana read the telegram. And after a moment's pause for thought, he answered slowly, "Well, no, I rather think not. When you have got an elephant by the hind leg and he's trying to run away, it's best to let him run."*

Lincoln's image regarding Thompson was valid. The Canadian Confederate leader was indeed a formidable foe—if only because the Union generals opposing him were such total asses. The Canadian government itself—and along with it the English —were bending over backward to remain neutral, but Union General John Dix was proving himself to be the Southerners' best ally. Though Lincoln had quietly chastised him for sending Union forces into Canada to pursue Bennett Young's raiders, Dix continued to play into the hands of the Confederates. He struck again, on December 14, 1864, with "General Orders No. 97":

> Information having been received at these headquarters . . . that other marauding enterprises of a like character are in preparation in Canada, the Commanding General deems

---

* Later, Dana spent that terrible night at the bedside of the dying President, leaving around three o'clock in the morning—when Lincoln was still alive—to go home for sleep. Shortly after eight o'clock in the morning he was awakened by a relentless knocking on his lower windowpane. It was Colonel Pelouze of the Adjutant General's office, who said, "Mr. Dana, the President is dead, and Mr. Stanton directs you to arrest Jacob Thompson."

it due to the people of the frontier towns to adopt the most prompt and efficient measures for the security of their lives and property. All military commanders on the frontiers are therefore instructed, in case further acts of depredation and murder are attempted, whether by marauders or persons acting under pretended commissions from the rebel authorities at Richmond, to shoot down the perpetrators, if possible, while in the commission of their crimes; or if it be necessary with a view to their capture to cross the boundary between the United States and Canada, said commanders are hereby directed to pursue them wherever they may take refuge; and, in the event of their capture, they are under no circumstances to be surrendered, but are to be sent to these headquarters for trial and punishment by martial law.

The *Times* of London called it "a declaration of war against Canada," and Senator Charles Sumner later described actions such as the St. Albans' raid as "a trap in which to catch the government of our country. It was hoped that in this way the rebellion would gain the powerful British intervention which would restore its failing fortunes . . ."

Lincoln quietly slapped Dix's hands for Order No. 97, but in the same month the President also issued orders requiring travelers along the border—for the first time—to possess passports.

Two days later, John Beall—of *Philo Parsons* fame—struck a third time.

Landlocked by the winter, on December 16, 1864, Beall tried unsuccessfully to derail a train bound for Buffalo—and was captured on the Union side of the Niagara bridge. He was brought before a military commission on two charges involving nine specifications, and on February 8, 1865, was adjudged guilty of both charges and of eight of the nine specifications.

The sentence of death was recommended.

It was necessary, under Union military law, for the commanding general to issue the final order for capital punishment. Unfortunately for Acting Master Beall, the commanding general was John A. Dix. He surprised no one by ordering that a gallows be built, and in setting the execution date for February 18, Dix felt compelled to write: "The Major General Commanding feels that a want of firmness and inflexibility on his part, in executing the sentence of death in such a case, would be an offense against the outraged citizenry and humanity of the age."

But there were other forces afoot.

Beall, a particularly popular young man in the South as well as among his comrades in Canada, was the son of a wealthy and socially prominent Virginia family. A mighty effort was begun to save him from the gallows.

Young, handsome and brave, John Beall became the Major André of the Civil War—and just as George Washington was reported to have wept over the young English spy's death, so would Lincoln be sorely pressured to offer clemency to Beall. Senator Orville H. Browning, a personal friend of the President, called on Lincoln to beg mercy, and presented a petition on behalf of the prisoner signed by ninety-one members of Congress. Postmaster-General Montgomery Blair, and even radical* Republican leader Thaddeus Stevens (who would later lead the impeachment forces against Andrew Johnson) sought leniency. Six U.S. senators formally petitioned Lincoln to commute Beall's sentence, noting that the young man was "regularly commissioned in the rebel service and that Jefferson Davis ... assumed all responsibility for his action."

With such powerful support behind his own humanitarian instincts—and with the war itself rapidly moving toward the complete collapse of the Confederate army—there was little reason to believe that Abraham Lincoln would do less than commute young Beall's sentence. There could be no contribution made to military victory by the killing of a captured spy—and in fact during this period Lincoln suspended the executions

---

* "Radical" was a term used to describe those men—usually Republicans—who planned to impose harsh conditions for readmittance to the Union on the formerly Confederate states.

of four other men, including one who had been condemned as a Confederate spy. But Acting Master Beall had become a pawn, rather than a man, in a very tight chess match.

On February 6, 1865, the Canadian Parliament had passed what would come to be called the "Alien Act," providing for the expulsion from that country of any foreigners suspected of engaging in warlike acts against a friendly nation, and along with it the levying of a $3,000 fine against any such persons. The act also called for the seizure of ships and arms intended for the use of such hostile persons.

Four days later, Bennett Young and his St. Albans' raiders—who had been freed once by a Canadian court—were dragged to a second trial. Canada's Parliament moved again, this time to appropriate $50,000 from its own money to reimburse the St. Albans' banks for the money Young's men had stolen, and in response to this act Lincoln began preparations to rescind the passport order. Both Canada and the United States undertook to post rewards for marauding Confederates.

Seward was winning the diplomatic war, but on both sides of the border public emotions continued to run high, and it was within this atmosphere that the governments of both the United States and Canada were required to work against heavy public pressure to avoid the trap the Confederate agents were doing their best to set.

To the Confederates in Canada, it was an alarming turn of events. Within the space of a year they had seen a well-financed mission with tacit Canadian support turn to a situation in which each member's head carried a price, and in which the gallows was a probable final destination. With the Southern armies collapsing, they could not even look to a possible salvation through undertaking the considerable dangers of a return journey to their homes in the South. They were trapped men in an alien and increasingly hostile land.

The likelihood of war between England and the Union was far from over—but it was lessening, and Seward was able to let it be known among the English that the Rush-Bagot Agreement might not be formally severed after all. But the same Congress that petitioned for Beall's life continued to prod Seward into a position of having to threaten rescinding the Rush-Bagot Agreement—and on the Canadian side the government was required to continue telling its people (and not without some truth) that the troops it was posting along the border with the United States were being stationed to repel an invasion as well as to arrest Confederates.

On February 18, William H. Seward, Secretary of State of the United States of America, was moving heaven and earth to work with the Canadians to put a stop to the border raids before an incident—such as the implementation of Dix's stupid pursuit orders—could ignite hostilities. He would be put into a difficult position, indeed, if the President of the United States himself refused to deal as seriously with the raiders as Mr. Secretary Seward wished the Canadians to do.

John Yates Beall was an admitted agent of the Confederate Commissioners. Seward was required to oppose any plea of leniency for Beall—and his argument would be a compelling one, even to Lincoln.

Thus Acting Master Beall would have to die in the cause of averting war with England, and such was the toll on Lincoln that Browning described him as more agitated over the young Confederate's death than he had ever known the President to be over anything before. "No man knows the distress of my mind," Lincoln said. "The case of Beall on the Lakes—there had to be an example. They tried me every way. They wouldn't give up. But I had to stand firm. I even had to turn away his poor sister when she came and begged for his life, and let him be executed, and he was executed, and I can't get the distress out of my mind yet."

Acting Master Beall went to the gallows on February 24, 1865, but his involvement with Seward and with Lincoln—the only two men attacked by assassins the evening of April 14,

1865—did not end with his death. For on February 21, Beall had taken pen in hand to address a letter to Jacob Thompson in Canada:

"Sir,
Perhaps I should have written you sooner, but I knew that you were not inappreciative of my situation, and I hope that you do not slacken your efforts on account of the reprieve of six days. You may not succeed in your efforts, but I do expect you to vindicate my character. I have been styled a pirate, robber, etc. When the United States' authorities, after such a 'trial' shall execute such a sentence, I do earnestly call on you to officially vindicate me at least to my countrymen. With unabated loyalty to our cause of self-government, and my country, and an earnest prayer for our success as a nation, and kindest feelings for yourself, I remain, truly, your friend,

John Yates Beall."

By early March, Seward and Lincoln had clearly won the diplomatic war. And on March 2, Confederate Secretary of State Judah P. Benjamin formally recalled the Confederate commissioners from Canada, thus adding to the hopelessness of the refugees the chaos of having their own government leaving them stranded.

Thompson himself, in the summer of 1864, had declared publicly that no act would be left unconsidered as a means of saving the South, including having Lincoln "put out of the way."* Now, without the restraint of even his formal leadership, the talk overheard at the Queen's Hotel grew more extreme—and much of it was directed against the two men who were the cause of all their troubles as well as Beall's: Abraham Lincoln and William H. Seward.

---

* The source of this quote was a perjurer—but one who was present in Montreal, and who was expanding upon truth rather than creating lies out of whole cloth. Jacob Thompson, for his part, could not leave Canada immediately after he was recalled. He appears to have remained at his post, and apparently banked $100,000 in the Confederate account during the first week of April 1865. He changed his plans to flee from Buffalo, and made good his escape to England from a Canadian port.

Soon John Beall's last letter became the subject of discussion, and many a witness heard the Confederates speak of it as being the young officer's cry that his own death be avenged. Within a month, in the gloom of the Queen's Hotel which followed the news of Lee's surrender on April 9, witnesses began hearing talk of "good news coming soon from Washington," mingled with curses against the two top Union officials, and on the rainy evening of April 14 a weary and sad Orville Browning wrote in his diary: "I am at a loss as to the class of persons who instigated the crime"; but he added the belief that they might be "the accomplices of Beall who was recently hung at New York. I am inclined to the latter opinion."

CHAPTER

VII

The Ultimate Border Incident

THE CABAL IN CANADA began going to pieces in the spring of 1865. Their mission officially ended with Thompson's recall in March, and they became increasingly dependent upon couriers for information and direction. John Harrison Surratt, Jr., aged twenty-three, spent the first days of April 1865 journeying from Richmond to Washington, and on April 3 Louis Weichmann greeted him in his mother's boardinghouse on H Street by saying: "Why, Surratt, I thought you'd gone to Richmond!"

Surratt exhibited a pocketful of twenty-dollar gold pieces, explaining that he had just come from the Confederate capital and that he was leaving next day for Montreal.

Weichmann asked him about the news—then on the lips of everyone in Washington—that the Confederacy had abandoned its capitol at Richmond.

"No!" came the vehement answer, "it has not! I saw Davis

The Ultimate Border Incident / 81

and Benjamin in Richmond, and they told me it would not be evacuated."

There were, however, other opinions.

> Head Quarters Armies of the United States
> City Point,
> April 2 7:45 AM 1865

Mrs. A. Lincoln
Washington, D.C.

Last night General Grant telegraphed that Sheridan with his cavalry and the Fifth Corps had captured three brigades of infantry, a train of wagons, and several batteries, prisoners amounting to several thousands. This morning General Grant, having ordered an attack along the whole line, telegraphs as follows: "Both Wright and Park got through the enemy's lines. The battle now rages furiously. Sheridan with his cavalry, the Fifth Corps, and Miles' Division of the Second Corps, which was sent to him since one this AM is now sweeping down from the west. All now looks highly favorable. Orders engaged but I have not yet heard the result in his front."

Robert* yesterday wrote a little cheerful note to Captain Penrose, which is all I have heard of him since you left. Copy to Secretary of War.

(Note: Actual cable is unsigned.)

> City Point Va. April 2, 1865

Mrs. Lincoln: At 4:30 PM today General Grant telegraphed that he had Petersburg completely enveloped from river below to river above, and has captured, since he started last Wednesday, about twelve thousand prisoners and fifty guns. He suggests that I shall go out and see him in the morning which I think I will do. Tad and I are both well and will be glad to see you and your party at the time you name.

> A. Lincoln

---

* Robert Todd Lincoln, the President's son, was an officer in the Union forces in Virginia. He later served as Secretary of War in the administration of James A. Garfield—the second President to die from an assassin's bullet.

> Head Quarters Armies of the United States
> City Point,
> April 3, 8/oo AM 1865
>
> Hon Sec. of War
> Washington, D.C.
>
> This morning Gen. Grant reports Petersburg evacuated; and he is confident Richmond also is. He is pushing forward to cut off if possible the retreating army. I start to him in a few minutes.
>
> A. Lincoln

ON APRIL 4, John Surratt left Washington for Montreal, apparently unaware that on that same day Abraham Lincoln was walking unguarded through the city of Richmond. Those who walked at the President's side remembered that the blacks called out his name and bowed down before him, to his considerable embarrassment, and called him their Messiah. The atmosphere was contagious: "When President Lincoln entered the town on the fourth he received a most enthusiastic reception from the inhabitants," General Weitzel wrote to Charles A. Dana. "The night after I arrived the theater opened."

LINCOLN AT LAST had an argument to use against his crepe-hanging friends in Washington; he had walked unguarded through Richmond, and had been welcomed. Surely he would be safe in Washington. Lamon and Stanton were countered, if not convinced. In fact, the President was in considerably more danger than even they realized. Jefferson Davis—a fugitive commanding still-dangerous troops—issued a proclamation soon after leaving Richmond in which he explained the South's defeat by claiming victory. With the fall of Richmond, the Confederate President said to his people, there was no longer a need to defend territory; now the troops were free to hit and to run, to hide in the daytime and strike back in the night's darkness, to fade away and emerge again to strike only when the enemy was vulnerable. It was a call to the Confederate nation to wage guerrilla war on a total scale.

"Let us but will it," Davis exhorted his troops, "and we are free."

Unwilling to surrender, Jefferson Davis now called for desperate measures. Long the foe of emancipation, he had in recent weeks approved sending an emissary to Europe empowered to promise that the Southern slaves would be freed even if the Confederacy won the war, and the man was escorted as far as Baltimore by two never-identified Confederate agents who traveled closely northward along the route John Wilkes Booth would follow in the opposite direction. On their way, the agents particularly remembered passing Surratt's Tavern.

NO DESCRIPTION of Washington in 1865 is complete without an understanding of the Maryland Peninsula. Separated from the South by the Potomac River and the Chesapeake Bay, it has always compensated for that accident of geography with an excess of southernness.

Throughout the Civil War, the Maryland Peninsula was an underground thoroughfare teeming with activity between Richmond and all of its sympathizers in the North. Everyone knew everyone else to be in the "conspiracy," and for those who didn't freely choose the Southern cause there was always the motivation provided by local bands of thugs who called themselves "guerrillas." Few men on the peninsula sympathized with the North, and of those who did, none publicized the fact.

Within that context, the Confederacy died harder in the peninsula than it did farther south. On the peninsula, it lived on conspiracy, rumor and hope—it had always lived under the reality of Union armies, and so it moved with more activity in the dark than in the daylight, as much so in terms of its information as its action. The evacuation of Richmond may have been a trauma in the South, but on the peninsula it changed things not a bit. The Union troops that had always been there were not increased. Couriers between Montreal and Richmond continued to move as freely as they had before. And the word from the Confederate officials was that the South could now fight more fiercely and effectively, since the capital needn't drain troops from the front for the defense of its own borders.

"We will return," Jefferson Davis wrote from Danville, Virginia, on April 3. "Let us, then, not despond, my countrymen, but relying on God, meet the foe with fresh defiance."

The Confederacy still fielded two major armies—Lee's in Virginia, and the forces under General Joseph E. Johnston, who had been beaten from Atlanta to North Carolina by Sherman, but who nevertheless remained formidable.

Toward the close of a chess match, however, the knights and pawns are freed of their roles to defend the more powerful pieces and, in attack, become dangerous themselves. Davis hoped to play his final moves recklessly, relying upon speed and bravado to overcome his opponents' more powerful position.*

NEITHER LEE NOR JOHNSTON was powerful enough to turn against either of their pursuers. The railroad from the Carolinas led north to Danville, Virginia, and from Richmond another railroad led south to Danville. Lee and Johnston moved along the tracks toward each other, hoping to merge their armies in Danville, where they would be fed and armed from the supplies which were concentrated there. Throughout the countryside, the people were to rise against every blue-clad soldier, sniping at him and destroying his provisions.

It was little more than an ambitious dream. Lee and Johnston had to move their armies along one hundred and twenty miles of railroad, without food or ammunition, against the closely following harassment of 180,000 well-supplied Union troops.

---

* At this point, Jefferson Davis was unquestionably behaving irrationally. The war was over; the only question left was how many more lives would be lost before Davis realized the war was over. His own irrationality perhaps gives us a clue to the states of mind of the men in Canada who, unlike their President, did not know the real fortunes of the war and the real status of the rebellion.

The Ultimate Border Incident / 85

Fast Union cavalry cut the tracks north of Johnston, and others did the same south of Lee. Johnston had no choice but to dig in, and Lee had no alternative but to turn from the south and move west toward the small town of Appomattox Courthouse.

STILL NOT PERSONALLY DEFEATED, Davis himself now fled Danville to take up a brief residence in Greensboro, North Carolina. His cabinet met with him there on April 12—with some notable absentees.

Assistant Secretary of War Archibald Campbell had remained behind in Richmond in March to greet Lincoln with entreaties to enter the military convention they had discussed at conferences earlier in the year. Word of the discussions had spread throughout both sides, and Campbell clung to its hopes like a drowning man to a twig.

Alexander Stephens—Vice-President of the Confederate States of America—had quit cold rather than be a party to what many considered to be the madness (in the clinical sense) of Jefferson Davis, whose policies at this stage of the war could be compared to those of another military dictator a century later who led another nation in the enslavement of a minority, and who, in the face of defeat, chose Götterdämmerung.

NO SUBTLETIES OF POLITICS, no careful planning to deal with the very real and present postwar problems could possibly be discussed with a man in such a state of mind as Jefferson Davis now occupied. A fugitive in flight for his freedom, and perhaps his life, Davis was giving orders as if he still commanded a nation and its regular armies. The regular armies knew better: on April 9 Robert E. Lee laid down his arms and Joe Johnston began bartering for terms.

BUT ON THE MARYLAND PENINSULA and in Washington, and along every resting place between Richmond and Canada, none of the reality was visible. On the peninsula all of the plots and schemes had relied upon Confederate hopes, not circumstances, and the same held true throughout the tunnel of committed men along the line from Richmond to Montreal. Reduced to issuing proclamations instead of orders, Jefferson Davis had many more things to worry over than misinterpretations of his orders among his irregulars behind the Union lines.

Wilkes was such an irregular, as were John Surratt and Jacob Thompson. All of them had once considered a scheme to kidnap the President of the United States—and had failed in it. They had also, separately and/or together, fomented a plot to burn New York and Baltimore, and had failed. All of the crackpot schemes had been tried—from shipping the clothes of yellow fever victims to the White House to fomenting revolution in the northwest to beating Lincoln in the election.

And it is easier to get away from a dead man than to spirit a live one past all of his troops.

Desperate men were looking for the bold stroke of history—pushed, all of them, by the proclamations of their accepted leader and President: "Let us but will it, and we are free."

In the first week of April 1865, John Surratt carried the last words of Jefferson Davis to the desperate men in Canada.

CHAPTER

VIII

"Long Live Our Chief, the President..."

IT WAS FIVE DAYS since Lee had surrendered his pitiful 9,000 men to Grant's 100,000 on the fields surrounding the little crossroads that was Appomattox, Virginia. It was five days since the large-scale killing had come to an end. Grant had lost 17,000 men in two days in The Wilderness; he had lost 5,000 in ten minutes at Cold Harbor. Among his predecessors, Burnside had left 13,000 behind at Fredericksburg, and under Meade and Lee, 51,000 from both sides were killed and maimed during three days at Gettysburg. And now—on Good Friday—it was done. Sherman still opposed Johnston's guns in North Carolina, but they were silent guns strung across the backs of retreating men, and they would be given up entirely within twelve days. Kirby Smith and Dick Taylor still answered only to Jefferson Davis, but they too would soon surrender their forces and return to their hopes and their crops and their families.

ON THIS TWENTY-FOURTH DAY of spring, 1865, the proprietors of Wolfsheimer & Bro. joined the rest of Washington in decorating their windows for celebration with the sign:

> Long live our chief, the President
> In glory, peace and health;
> Nobly he brought the war to end,
> Crushed treason in its wealth
> O God! preserve his worthy life,
> Let never war or civil strife
> Again disturb our land.

On that same day, in South Carolina, Major Robert Anderson rowed a small boat across the choppy waters of Charleston harbor. Tucked under his arm was a flag—the same flag he had watched being lowered from its mast exactly four years earlier. Four years to the day since the accuracy of Beauregard's gray-clad batteries from The Citadel and a lack of supplies had compelled him to surrender his command at Fort Sumter. Now he was returning, to raise the flag again as if, after four years of slaughter, nothing had changed.

THE DAY WAS APRIL 14, 1865, and The War was over. The battles to be fought around its name would come—the struggles to view it as "The War of Rebellion," or "The War for Southern Independence," or "The War Between the States," or simply as "The Civil War." The struggles of hate and political power and racial arrogance were yet to be fought; the struggle of tears and blood was finally over.

The agony and the killing were done. Casualty lists from victories at Gettysburg and Vicksburg would come no more— the painful victories. The lists from defeats at Fredericksburg and Manassas would come no more—the painful defeats. No more would Americans see the battlefield hospitals, the "building lighted partially with candles. All around . . . lay the wounded men, some cursing and swearing and some praying; in the middle of the room there was some ten or twelve tables with just enough room to lay a man on; these were used as dissecting tables and they were covered with blood . . . By the side of the tables was a heap of feet, legs, and arms."

No more filthy stench would surround the tents full of the maimed and the dying as they writhed in agony for the merciful relief of either chloroform or death. No more graves and crutches would scar the Land of Opportunity.

At Ford's New Theatre that day, final preparations were being made for the President's evening visit. John T. Ford himself was out of town when it was first learned that the President planned to attend the Good Friday performance of *Our American Cousin*, but it would no doubt have pleased him that just two days before his own thirty-sixth birthday the President would give his theatre the honor of his first visit since Lee's surrender.

Rumor had originally indicated that the honor would be served upon Grover's Theater, and as a matter of fact, on April 13 the manager of Grover's, C. D. Hess, had penned an invitation to the First Couple. Hess would later remember that he was reminded to do so by the famous actor, John Wilkes Booth. "He seated himself in a chair," Hess remembered, "and entered into a conversation on the general illumination of the city that night."*

"He asked me if I intended to illuminate. I said yes, I should,

---

* In celebration of the end of the war, residents of the city of Washington had determined to string the streets of the capital city with transparencies, Japanese lanterns, and whatever else could be set aglow from within by candle, oil, or kerosene fires. The city was consequently decorated like a Christmas tree; but to the Confederate sympathizers in Washington it would have had the same effect as confronting a fighting bull with all the red capes of Mexico and Spain.

to a certain extent; but that the next night would be my great night of the illumination, that being the celebration of the fall of Sumter."

"Do you intend to invite the President?" Booth asked casually.

"Yes," Hess answered, and then added quickly, "That reminds me; I must send that invitation."

But it was to Ford's New Theatre that the messenger was dispatched from the White House at ten-thirty the next morning. "A young man, a messenger from the White House, came and engaged the box," Dick Ford recalled later. "The President had been previously invited to the theatre that night, and I had no knowledge of his intention to visit the theatre until the reception of that message."

Dick Ford's brother Harry arrived from his breakfast shortly after the messenger had left, and the two men discussed the propriety of advertising the President's attendance in order to attract a larger crowd to the performance. Deciding to publicize the information, they wrote a notice for the *Evening Star* and sent it off immediately by messenger. At the same time, Dick Ford left to personally carry a similar message to the offices of the *National Republican*.

John Ford—the owner of the theatre, who employed his two brothers to manage it—had known Wilkes since the actor's "childhood, and intimately for six or seven years." Consequently, the young actor made of Ford's Theatre a virtual home-away-from-home, and John Ford would recall later that "I seldom visited the theatre but what I found him about or near it, during the day, while I was there. I usually came down to the theatre three days a week, devoting the other three to my business in Baltimore, and being there between the hours of ten and three. I would nearly always meet Booth there when I was in the city. He had his letters directed to the theatre, and that was the cause of his frequent visits there...."

Shortly after younger brother Dick left for the *National*

Republican offices, Harry Ford saw Wilkes coming up the street to the theatre. Popular as ever, despite his long absence from the stage, Booth was merrily greeted upon the steps of Ford's by several other theatre men, one of whom went inside to get a letter addressed to Booth. "He sat on the steps while reading his letter," Ford remembered, "every now and then looking up and laughing."

A few days before, John Surratt had written John Wilkes Booth from Canada.

"It was while Booth was there," Harry Ford recalled, "that I suppose he learned of the President's visit to the theatre that evening."

Leaving the theatre, Booth passed Dick Ford at the corner of E and 10th Streets, continued on to Pumphrey's Livery Stables, and made arrangements to pick up a rented horse around four o'clock that afternoon.

Meanwhile, at Naylor's Stables, another horse deal was going on. David Herold and George Atzerodt asked Naylor's foreman to board a dark-bay mare with which they arrived at about one o'clock. At the same time Fletcher took the dark bay, he arranged with Herold to rent him a different horse, which Herold would pick up around four o'clock.

Across Pennsylvania Avenue, at 12th Street, on an angle from Naylor's, stood the Kirkwood Hotel—in which were registered both Vice President Andrew Johnson and, as of that morning, George Atzerodt. At about one o'clock the Kirkwood's day clerk, Robert Jones, saw both Herold and Atzerodt as they stood talking at the main counter. Curiously, no witness could recall actually renting the room to Atzerodt, but a host of incriminating articles would later be found in the room rented in his name. These included a black coat hung on a wall, its pockets containing a bank book in the name of John Wilkes Booth, recording a credit of $455 with the Ontario Bank, Montreal, and alongside it a map of Virginia. A loaded and capped revolver was found under a pillow on the bed. Other items included a handkerchief marked with the name of Booth's mother, and a bowie knife, found between the sheets of the bed.

Sometime during that day, the Kirkwood's clerk would be handed a card which he would put into the box of Vice President Johnson's secretary, William A. Browning; it read: "Don't wish to disturb you; are you at home?" The card was signed "J. Wilkes Booth."

Meanwhile, John Wilkes Booth spent the early portion of that afternoon in Lewis Powell's room at the Herndon House, and he was not seen elsewhere in the city until shortly past two o'clock. In the meantime, Atzerodt was seen at Howard's Stables trying unsuccessfully to engage yet another saddle horse, and later at Kelleher's Stable, where he gave the names of several persons in Maryland and Washington as references and then paid five dollars to rent "a small bay mare, 16½ hands high." James Kelleher remembered the time of the transaction as being around two-thirty in the afternoon.

The man who had seen Atzerodt at Howard's was Louis Weichmann, who had gone there on the instructions of his landlady, Mary Surratt, to engage a buggy. "She herself gave me the money on that occasion, a ten-dollar note, and I paid six dollars for the buggy. I drove her to Surrattsville that same day, arriving there about half-past four."

But Mrs. Surratt had a visitor around two o'clock—just before she left, Weichmann would recall. "Just before leaving the city, as I was going to the door, I saw Mr. Booth in the parlor and Mrs. Surratt was speaking with him. They were alone. He did not remain in the parlor more than three or four minutes; and immediately after he left, Mrs. Surratt and I left."

Weichmann, by happenstance, was with John Surratt nearly a month earlier when the young Confederate agent had rented the Herndon House room for Powell which Booth had left just prior to the conversation with Mrs. Surratt.

One witness, a barber, would later claim that John Surratt and John Wilkes Booth had come to his establishment on the morning of April 14 to be shaved. He would positively identify John Surratt by sight as having been in his shop that morning. Another witness saw John Surratt—at about the same time Weichmann saw Booth conversing with Mrs. Surratt—passing the National Theater. "We bowed to each other as he passed," said David Reed, adding, "I have known John Surratt a great while. I knew him when quite a boy, at his father's house, and have seen him out gunning." His "father's house" was the tavern in Maryland to which Louis Weichmann was taking Surratt's mother. With her she was carrying a pair of binoculars that would later be among the possessions confiscated at Garrett's farm, after Wilkes Booth died there.

John Wilkes Booth himself was seen shortly before three o'clock just in front of Ford's Theatre.

"See what a nice horse I have got," the actor said to James P. Ferguson, who owned the restaurant adjoining the north side of Ford's. "Now watch, he can run just like a cat."

Two others saw him at about the same time, in the alley behind the theatre, where Booth rented a small stable. Mary Jane Anderson—a black woman—remembered: "I stood in my gate and looked right wishful at him," as Booth "and this lady were pointing up and down the alley as if they were talking about it. They stood there a considerable time, and then Booth went into the theatre." John Miles, who worked at the theatre, recalled that "about three o'clock in the afternoon Booth put his horse in the stable and Ned Spangler and Jim Maddox were with him. The stable is not more than five yards from the theatre."

Ford's assistant property man, John Sleichmann, saw Booth on the afternoon of the 14th, between four and five o'clock, in the restaurant next door. "I went in to look for James Maddox, and I saw Booth, Ned Spangler, Jim Maddox, Peanuts, and a young gentleman by the name of James Mouldey, I think, drinking there."

While Booth and his cronies were enjoying their glasses,

Harry Ford was busy inside the theatre decorating the special boxes President Lincoln and his party would use that evening. The Presidential Box at Ford's New Theatre was actually created by removing a partition which normally separated Boxes Seven and Eight. From the vantage point of a person seated in the audience, the box seats available at Ford's could be seen flanking the stage, with Boxes One and Two at stage level to the left with Three and Four above them, and balanced by Boxes Five and Six rising from the stage to the audience's right, with Seven and Eight stacked above them. Removing the partition separating Box Seven from Box Eight gave the President's party a wedge-shaped box at balcony level just directly above the stage, and while Lincoln could be seen by many people in the audience, he would still enjoy relative privacy.

The boxes themselves, in John Ford's opinion, were actually among the worst seats in the house, requiring their patrons to lean over the railing to watch the actors during any activity at their own end of the stage. With his usual candor, the impresario noted that the only reason for constructing the boxes at all was because Washington audiences were sufficiently interested in the prestige of a private box to put up with the poor view.

Since the ledge of the Presidential Box stood some eight feet or so above the stage, it could be entered only from the balcony. A visitor would have to approach the outer door by the main passageway of the balcony. Inside that outer door was a very short and narrow hallway, perhaps five feet long and three feet wide, which led to the twin inner doors opening into Boxes Seven and Eight. Cramped so closely together that their latches almost touched, the doors stood at right angles to one another. The door to the right of a man facing them normally led into Box Eight, and the door to the left into Box Seven. With the partition removed, the Box Eight door led to the rear of the Presidential Box, with the left-hand door opening directly into the front corner nearest the audience.

For tight security, normally the outer door could be locked and a guard stationed in the little hallway. But the locks to both the outer door and the door to Box Seven had been broken some weeks earlier, so Harry Ford had one of his workmen build a wedge to secure the outer door from the inside, on the theory that the guard could use the bar to insure himself against surprise. A small niche was therefore carved into the wall, and a length of board cut to the correct size to be jammed into place between the inward-opening door and the wall. Any visitor would have to satisfy the guard about the purity of his intention before entering the hallway. If the guard was posted outside the door, rather than condemned to spending nearly three hours in the closet-sized passage, the Lincoln party itself could secure the door as a second line of defense.*

The regular furniture was removed from the boxes in honor of the President's visit, and Harry Ford replaced it with three velvet-covered armchairs, a matching velvet-covered sofa and a cane chair. A stagehand was sent to bring an upholstered walnut rocker from John Ford's own apartment on the third floor above the Star Saloon next door, for the President's own use.

When the final arrangements had been made, there was a velvet-cushioned chair positioned in the front corner farthest from the audience, upon which Clara Harris, the Lincolns' guest, would sit during the performance. Her fiancé, Major Henry R. Rathbone, would sit upon the sofa located next to her chair, holding her hand. At the other end of the sofa, sitting upon the cane chair, would be Mary Todd Lincoln, holding the hand of her husband. The two couples would occupy a line at the front of the box, with the two remaining velvet chairs at the rear. During the early parts of the play, President Lincoln's valet would occupy one of them.

John Ford's own rocker, brought from his apartment, would

---

* The theory that Booth prepared this wedge in advance of the crime was hotly contested by the last relative of the Ford family, in correspondence with the author and others.

occupy the corner of the box nearest the audience. Abraham Lincoln would sit upon it.

Good Friday, April 14, 1865, held patriotic as well as religious significance in the Union—four years earlier to the day, Fort Sumter had fallen to begin the war—and all of Washington was decorating itself in celebration of the war's end. For his part, Harry Ford was not about to be upstaged in the decoration category, and he placed two American flags on staffs at each end of the Presidential Box and draped two more on the velvet-covered railings of each of the two boxes. At the centerpost he had workmen hang a blue regimental flag of the Treasury Guards for color, and underneath he instructed the workmen to hang a gilt-framed portrait of George Washington.

WHILE HARRY FORD BUSIED HIMSELF completing the preparations of the Presidential Box, Wilkes paid his second visit to James Pumphrey's livery stable, planning to pick up the horse he had engaged earlier in the day. Pumphrey remembered that Booth had expected to rent a sorrel horse he had been in the habit of riding. "But that horse was engaged," said Pumphrey, and he had in its place a small bay mare about fourteen or fourteen and a half hands high.

"She was a bay, with black legs, black mane and tail, and a white star in the forehead. . . . I have never seen the mare since."

Booth asked Pumphrey for a tie rein, and "I told him not to hitch her, as she was in the habit of breaking the bridle." Booth repeated his request for a tie rein, saying he wanted to stop by a restaurant for a drink.

"Get a boy at the restaurant to hold her," answered Pumphrey, holding his ground.

After sparring unsuccessfully a bit more over the tie rein, Booth said, "I'm going to Grover's Theater to write a letter; there's no necessity of tying her there, for there is a stable in the back part of the alley and I'll put her there." Then he asked

Pumphrey if he had any good ideas where he might ride around for a while.

"You've been some time around here, and you ought to know."

"How is Crystal Spring?"

"A very good place," Pumphrey answered, "but it's rather early for it."

"Well, I'll go there after I get through writing a letter."

Instead of Grover's, Booth went to the National Hotel at 6th Street and Pennsylvania Avenue, where he maintained rooms, and asked the desk clerk if he could use the office to write a letter. The clerk would later testify that Booth appeared to be dazed when he asked for privacy in which to write, and even inquired what year it was.

Whether or not it was an act, Booth appeared in perfectly fine mettle a short while later when an old friend and fellow actor, John Matthews, spoke with him on Pennsylvania Avenue.* Wilkes asked Matthews to take a letter and deliver it next morning to the editor of the *National Intelligencer*. Later that night Matthews would destroy the letter after reading it, forgetting all the contents except that, at the bottom, John Wilkes Booth had signed his own name along with those of Herold, "Payne," and Atzerodt.

As Wilkes and Matthews talked that afternoon on Pennsylvania Avenue, a carriage rolled past and both men recognized General Grant inside it. Booth hurriedly mounted and spurred his horse to the next block, to the front of the carriage, and peered inside.† The handbills issued by Dick and Harry Ford had proclaimed that Ulysses S. Grant would accompany Lin-

---

* In his own dreams for years afterwards, Matthews would remember a night when he had entertained John Wilkes Booth in the boardinghouse room Matthews had once occupied opposite Ford's Theatre. He would remember that his friend had been exhausted, and that their conversation had taken place while Wilkes lay flat upon his back, occupying the only mattress in the room. Matthews would remember it because Abraham Lincoln died upon that same bed.

† Grant's later memory of a strange and desperate-looking man chasing

coln to the theater that night, and Booth must have been taken aback to see the general riding toward the railroad terminal instead. Few in Washington knew that because Mrs. Grant and Mrs. Lincoln could barely abide one another, the general had given his excuses to the President and begged out of the invitation. He and his wife, Grant had explained, needed to take the train to New Jersey to visit their children.

AT APPROXIMATELY FOUR-THIRTY in the afternoon, at the Herndon House, Lewis Powell—registered as Lewis Payne—asked for an early supper, paid his bill in full, and checked out. In Surrattsville, Mrs. Surratt was at that hour telling her tenant, John Lloyd, to take the binoculars and to "have the shooting irons ready."

At the Kirkwood House, Vice-President Johnson's secretary absent-mindedly looked over John Wilkes Booth's calling card, mused that the famous actor might be remembering him from their acquaintanceship of years before, and assumed the card was for himself rather than for his boss.

"Between five and six o'clock that day," stagehand Joe Simms later recalled, "I was in front of the theatre when I saw Booth go into the restaurant by the side of the theatre. Spangler was sitting out in front, and Booth invited him to have a drink. I did not hear a word spoken between them."

During that same hour, Peanuts Burroughs remembered John Wilkes Booth bringing his horse to the special stable behind the theatre. "He hallooed out for Spangler," Peanuts would recall, and "when he came Booth asked him for a halter. He had none, and sent Jake upstairs after one."

Spangler argued with the actor to let him take the saddle off the horse, according to Peanuts, "but Booth wouldn't let him;

---

after his carriage would become "evidence" that an assassin had been sent after the general as well as the President.

then he wanted to take the bridle off, but Booth would not agree to it, so Spangler just put a halter round the horse's neck, but he took the saddle off afterward."

This is the second bay horse John Wilkes Booth has been seen riding during the day. Among the conspirators, three horses have been involved so far in the day's activities.

Atzerodt mounted a dark bay mare about one o'clock at Naylor's Stables.

An hour later, Atzerodt rented a small bay mare at Kelleher's Stable.

Two and one half hours after that, Booth rented a small bay from Pumphrey.

What was going on with the horses is a mystery with no answers. Atzerodt returned his rented bay to Kelleher's around nine-thirty that night, and then picked up the lodged bay from Naylor's an hour later. Booth will steal the Pumphrey horse for his escape, and David Herold returned to Naylor's at about four-thirty to pick up his own rented roan—which he would also steal for the getaway.

"At a quarter past four he came and asked me how much I would charge for the hire of the horse. I told him five dollars," said John Fletcher, the manager at Naylor's. "He wanted it for four. I told him he could not have it for that. He knew the horse, and inquired for that particular one. I went down to the stable with him, and told him to take a mare that was in the stable; but he would not have her. I then told him I would give him the other horse."

"He then wanted to see the saddles and bridles. I showed him a saddle and he said it was too small. Then I showed him another. That suited him very well, only that it had not the kind of stirrups he wanted. The stirrups were covered with leather, and he wanted a pair of English steel stirrups. He then wanted to see the bridles. I took him into the office and showed him the bridles, and he picked out a double-reined bridle. Before he mounted the horse, he asked me how late he could stay out with him. I told him he could stay out no later than eight o'clock, or nine at furthest."

HEROLD HAS SHOWN PARTICULAR CARE about the horse and equipment he has just rented from the stable where Atzerodt had earlier boarded a horse—and Herold has shown an interest in keeping the horse he plans to steal out later than normal. Wilkes has been seen riding a "small bay" matching the description of the horse Atzerodt rented from Kelleher's, and preceding the time Booth picked up his own horse from Pumphrey. Meantime, someone has left a lot of evidence—including Booth's bank book—in Atzerodt's room at the Kirkwood Hotel, and has left a calling card from John Wilkes Booth for Andrew Johnson or his private secretary, both of whom kept rooms at the Kirkwood. Booth has left a letter for a newspaper, and signed it with his name and the names of Herold, "Payne," and Atzerodt.

Those are the facts—and logic would suggest that Herold's chances of being out late with his rented horse might be improved if his friend Atzerodt had left a horse at the same stable for boarding, and therefore useful as security; logic would also suggest that Wilkes' chances of escaping might be improved if the descriptions of his horse were based upon the small bay Atzerodt rented, rather than upon the horse he really planned to ride—and it should not be forgotten that Pumphrey ended up saddling a small bay for Booth only because the horse the actor originally planned to rent was unavailable.

Add to these clues the evidence left behind in Atzerodt's room, and the German begins to look like a classic pigeon.

Add to everything else the fact that a map of Virginia was among the clues left in Atzerodt's room, and the fact that Atzerodt's primary usefulness to the Southern cause had come from the clandestine ferryboat he operated across the Potomac into Virginia, and the logic becomes almost a compelling argument that Atzerodt is being used to provide a string of misleading clues. To have Atzerodt in Washington, rather than waiting beside his boat on the shores of the Potomac, was to cut off the best and safest escape route to the South.

To have planted a coat in Atzerodt's room containing both a bank book in his own name and a map of Virginia would have been gross stupidity if Booth had in fact planned to go toward Virginia. And there would be no reason other than senseless treachery for Booth's signing Atzerodt's name to the *National Intelligencer* letter or to leaving his own calling card for Vice-President Johnson at the Kirkwood if Booth was not, in fact, trying to draw the attention of the authorities to Atzerodt's room at the Kirkwood and the clues planted there for them to find, leading the pursuers south to Virginia while the assassin escaped in a different direction.

And if poor George Atzerodt was to be set up for the gallows, then why not also use him to provide cover for stealing a couple of horses?

Leaving the restaurant where he was having drinks with Spangler, Booth was next seen about seven-thirty holding a horse at the rear of the theatre and calling out, "Ned! Ned! Ned!" When Spangler arrived, Booth said, "Tell Maddox to come here," and then left his horse with Maddox and entered the theatre. Having boarded Pumphrey's bay in the stable, Booth is leaving Kelleher's for Atzerodt to pick up.

Shortly afterwards, John Fletcher returned to his stable from supper to find Atzerodt having the boarded horse saddled and bridled. "He told me not to take the bridle or saddle off the mare until ten o'clock, and to keep the stable open for him. I said I would do so, and that I would be there myself at that time."

About eighty-thirty, Weichmann and Mrs. Surratt arrived back at the boardinghouse. "About ten minutes after we got back, someone rang the front doorbell," Weichmann remembered later. "It was answered by Mrs. Surratt, and I heard footsteps go into the parlor, immediately go out again, and down the steps. I was taking supper at the time."

As Weichmann ate, Abraham Lincoln had less than two hours to live.

CHAPTER

IX

The Secretary's Medicine

ABRAHAM LINCOLN was walking through the streets of Richmond on April 6, 1865, when an urgent telegram was sent to him from Washington.

"About two hours ago Mr. Seward was thrown from his carriage, his shoulder bone at the head of the joint broken off, his head and face much bruised, and he is, in my opinion, dangerously injured," Secretary of War Stanton had hurriedly wired the President. "I think your presence here is needed."

The horses had bolted precisely at the moment when the Secretary of State had begun to enter the carriage, and they had careened through the streets of Washington while he tried—heroically—to recapture the reins they had jerked loose before bolting. Seward was thrown hard from the runaway carriage, and those who reached him first believed he could not recover.

Immediately upon hearing of the accident, the President

began preparations to return to the capital. Spending the night at City Point, he wired General Grant on the morning of April 7: "General Sheridan says, 'If the thing is pressed I think that Lee will surrender. Let the thing be pressed.'" There were negotiations going on for the restoration of Virginia to the Union about which Seward had cabled the President before the accident—and Lincoln was underscoring an earlier instruction to Grant that "nothing I have done, or probably shall do, is to delay, hinder, or interfere with you in your work." The President was taking no chances that rumor would vitiate his understanding with Grant that military victory should under no circumstances be delayed until Lincoln could get Congress in line.*

In Washington, Seward was in agonizing pain. Immediately upon his arrival in the capital, the President visited his Secretary of State, and he returned frequently. Seward spoke little, primarily because his jaws were linked together by surgically placed wires on the inside, and a steel and plaster cast on the outside, holding the bones together until the fractures healed. The pain inside his broken skull kept him awake nights, leaving him exhausted and nearly comatose during the days. The shades were kept drawn to aid his rest in the top-rear bedroom of the three-story brick house across Lafayette Park from the White House.

The days passed for Seward in fleeting moments of blurred vision: sometimes he would see Lincoln beside his bed, at other times Edwin Stanton, and most frequently of all his daughter,

* Lincoln would if possible try to bring the Confederate States into the government without malice, but if military power was the only way, then this supremely competent politician would deal with that exigency as well. No matter his personal feelings about the matter, the President's policy was based on the premise that the sooner the nation was united once again, the more quickly it could return to building its future. (There were those cynics who noted that the million-member army could serve quiet occupation duty in the South or, on the other hand, could speed up Manifest Destiny with a quick military trip to Canada.) But a bit more of a delay would not really, in the larger scheme of things, make that all-fired much difference.

Fanny—babying him one moment and dashing for medicine the next.

Lincoln now had to work alone on the nation's international problems, save for advice received from time to time at Seward's bedside, but with Lee's defeat it became possible to rescind the blockade proclamations that had so nearly caused war with England.

Nine days after the carriage accident, the President of the United States took a breather. An idiotic farce at Ford's Theatre—a current hit—offered a night's vacation, and after everyone else had turned him down—notably the Stantons, because the Secretary of War disapproved of the President exposing himself to the danger of crowds; and the Grants, because Mrs. Grant could not long abide the company of Mary Lincoln —the President had succeeded in dragging along a minor military aide and his fiancée. Seward would later cryptically announce that "if I had known he was going, he would never have gone." But Seward was comatose.

A little after ten o'clock, as the President rocked in his box at the theatre, two men rode down 15½ Street and stopped before William Seward's home opposite Lafayette Park. The smaller man was a former druggist's clerk, David Herold, and it was probably his idea that the bigger man carry a small pharmacy package in his hand to facilitate entry into the sick man's home.

Lewis Powell also carried a pistol and a bowie knife.

INSIDE WILLIAM SEWARD'S HOME, his daughter Fanny was taking her turn watching over him until she would be relieved at eleven o'clock by her brother, Major Augustus Seward. With her in her father's room was George T. Robinson, a black soldier who had been wounded in action and who was assigned during his recuperation to nursing duty for Seward. Another brother, Assistant Secretary of State Frederick Seward, was up and about, and somewhere in the city a State Department messenger named Hansell was on his way to the Seward home with dispatches.

Five men and one woman were minutes away from meeting Lewis Powell, the Baptist preacher's kid.

WILLIAM BELL, the Seward family's black servant, answered the knock at the door and found himself staring up at a giant.

"Medicine from Dr. Verdi," Powell explained, holding up the package he had been given by David Herold. "I have orders to give it personally to Mr. Seward." The big man stepped across the threshold easily as Bell retreated, and was quickly inside the house.

Perhaps, Bell suggested while closing the door, it would be just as well to leave the medicine.

"Got to give it to him personally," Powell repeated.

William Bell later recalled that the big man "seemed to be excited and talked very fast and very loud." He couldn't remember the exact words, but it was a repeated line that Dr. Verdi insisted the medicine be given only to the Secretary himself. Powell kept moving forward all the time, Bell remembered, and clanged hard on the stairway steps. It was a curious parade—Powell in front, his boots hard and fast on the steps, and Bell behind shushing him—that came to an abrupt halt before Fred Seward, who asked just what in the hell was going on.

Powell again explained that Dr. Verdi had given him both the medicine and instructions to see that it was given to no one but Secretary of State Seward. Frederick offered to take the medicine.

Powell said he couldn't hand over the medicine, and Frederick suggested that in that event, perhaps it would be better if the messenger left and returned in the morning. The last thing Frederick Seward expected was an assassin. All he perceived was a stubborn, well-dressed intruder.

Powell turned away and appeared to move back downstairs, and William Bell, mistakenly assuming that he was now leading the parade, turned to lead the way back to the front door. Instead of the sound of heavy boots descending, however, Bell heard a click—followed by hammering sounds—and turned too late to observe what had happened.

Fred Seward lived—barely—to explain it: "Suddenly, turning again, he sprang up and forward, having drawn a Navy revolver which he leveled, with a muttered oath, and pulled the trigger . . ."

INSIDE THE SEWARDS' BEDROOM Fanny Seward and George Robinson heard the heavy boots come upstairs and then were unable to make out the muffled whispers of the conversation. The gas jets in the room were turned as low as possible to permit a fair amount of sight with minimum disturbance of the Secretary of State's sleep.

"Wouldn't you think that person would be more quiet coming to a sickroom?" Robinson said to Fanny.

Outside the door, Powell's pistol had misfired, aimed pointblank at Fred Seward's heart; and the old guerrilla had immediately turned it into a club, the first blow smashing through the skull and the second pushing the hole even more deeply into Fred Seward's brain.

ROBINSON PULLED OPEN THE DOOR, his angry voice raised to command silence, but the silhouette in the door paralyzed him for a long moment.

Moving at last, the Union soldier lunged at Powell and was sent reeling, his forehead slashed open. Fanny Seward grabbed at the attacker and was knocked across the room with a single powerful blow. Powell paused for a moment, his eyes groping against the new darkness until they found Seward's bed shoved against a far wall. Then he sprang forward.

SEWARD SAW THE HORROR slash first at his nurse and then at his daughter—watched it stand and pause to seek him out—and then helplessly raised a useless, defenseless arm as Powell leaped against him, grappling and pulling and slashing.

Climbing back to their feet, Robinson and Fanny dashed for the assassin, grabbing and clutching at him and pulling him away as Seward himself writhed helplessly between Powell and his daughter. The bowie knife cut down hard, nearly amputating Seward's entire cheek; then it slashed again, swiping from left to right along his throat, cutting deep into both sides even while being turned away from the jugular by the steel and plaster cast. Seward was swallowing blood now as Powell grabbed at his hair and began stabbing into the bedclothes, Seward rolling one way as Fanny and Robinson pulled Powell the other, and the knife sinking again and again into the rumpled bedding.

IN THE HALLWAY Augustus Seward came running, half asleep, toward the commotion. And at last Lewis Powell was pulled off the Secretary of State and shoved toward escape only as Augustus appeared, blocking the exit. "I'm mad! I'm mad!" Powell screamed as he shoved Fanny away a second time and began running toward the doorway. "I'm mad! I'm mad! Mad! Mad! Mad!"

Augustus was nearly scalped by a single knife slash as Powell clawed his way to the landing and leaped down the stairs.

WILLIAM BELL had begun running for the doorway when Frederick was attacked, and at the sight of him David Herold had run away. Both men's paths crossed Hansell's, but the State Department messenger did not understand what the excitement was all about. Therefore, with a bureaucrat's doggedness, he entered the open door and began quietly mounting the steps.

"I'm mad! Mad! Mad!" A specter in front of him screamed, and Hansel found himself suddenly a figure in slow motion, helpless to move as Powell's hand lifted high above him and arced downward, shoving the bowie knife's blade deeply into his chest.

Hansel dropped to the stairway while Powell continued toward the door.

"THOUGH THE SCENES of horror through which I have passed have neither hardened my heart nor paralyzed my hand," Mrs. William H. Seward wrote later, "I still find it difficult to guide my pen. . . . Robinson, the nurse, tried to prevent his entrance, was struck a number of times with a large bowie knife but still kept hold of that murderer while he sprang upon Mr. Seward's bed. Mr. Seward . . . says he knew the man sought his life, still he feared for Fanny, and, with great effort, rose up in his bed to interpose his shattered frame as a protection.

"His throat was cut on both sides, his right cheek nearly severed from his face, when he fell upon the floor. . . .

"In the meantime, Fanny's screams had awakened the family. Augustus, with the aid of Robinson, succeeded in getting the man out of the room. Augustus received three wounds from that fearful knife. His head was cut twice to the bone, and one hand severely cut. . . .

"I will not attempt to describe what I witnessed of this scene of horror. Mr. Seward and Frederick both insensible; and Augustus, Robinson, and Hansel covered with blood. Anna, with remarkable presence of mind, sent the servants for surgeons, who soon came."

There were those who would hold that William Bell showed the evening's best presence of mind. Passing Hansel on the porch, he had run out into the street, grabbing person after person and yelling, "Murderer! Murderer! Murderer!"

Seeing Bell, David Herold* left 15½ Street and headed toward escape. Powell's horse was left behind, and no doubt it joined like-minded humans who watched and listened to Bell but made no move.

Lewis Powell erupted from the Seward front door in a hurry and moved to his mount. After mounting the horse, he walked it away—perhaps because he was a calculating and cool killer, or perhaps because he was a confused man waiting for David Herold to come from the shadows to join him; but behind him, running as fast as his legs would move, William Bell ran and yelled, "Murderer! Murderer! Murderer!"

Curious, a crowd gathered as the little parade moved away from the carnage at the Seward home; and William Bell turned back again only after Powell, upon reaching Pennsylvania Avenue, gouged his spurs into the horse. Before the doorway he had left in his search for help, Bell now found a crowd of soldiers and civilians gawking and shoving.

He pushed his way inside, and there he found Hansel moaning on the stairway, Frederick barely sensible on the landing, and inside Secretary Seward's room, Robinson, Augustus, and the Secretary himself clumped over individual pools of their own blood.

SURGEON GENERAL BARNES was leaving his offices that night when he was summoned to the Seward home. There he met Dr. Verdi and Secretary of the Navy Gideon Welles.

"Hurrying forward into 15th Street," Welles wrote in his diary, "I found it pretty full of people, especially so near the residence of Secretary Seward for many soldiers as well as citizens gathered.

---

* If Wilkes killed Lincoln because only a famous actor could get close enough, then Davie Herold, the druggist's clerk, was a natural to accompany Powell in the preliminaries of the assault on the Secretary of State. Herold, not Powell, would know how prescriptions should be delivered. Even more important, Herold's familiarities with Washington streets would make him an invaluable guide for Powell during the escape.

"Entering the house, I found the lower hall and office full of persons, and among them most of the Foreign Legations, all anxiously inquiring what truth there was in the horrible rumors afloat. . . .

"The servants were frightened and appeared relieved to see me. I hastily asked what truth there was in the story that an assassin or assassins had entered the house and assaulted the Secretary. They said it was true, and that Mr. Frederick was also badly injured. They wished me to go up, but no others. At the head of the first stairs I met the elder Mrs. Seward [the Secretary's wife], who was scarcely able to speak but desired me to proceed up to Mr. Seward's room. I met Mrs. Frederick Seward [the Secretary's daughter-in-law] on the third story who, although in extreme distress, was, under the circumstances, exceedingly composed. I asked for the Secretary's room, which she pointed out, the southwest room. As I entered I met Miss Fanny Seward, with whom I exchanged a single word, and proceeded to the foot of the bed. Dr. Verdi and, I think, two others were there. The bed was saturated with blood. The Secretary was lying on his back, the upper part of his face covered with a cloth which extended down over his eyes. His mouth was open, the lower jaw dropping down. I exchanged a few whispered words with Dr. Verdi. Secretary Stanton, who came after but almost simultaneously with me, made inquiries in a louder tone until admonished by a word from one of the physicians. We almost immediately withdrew and went into an adjoining front room where lay Frederick Seward. . . . Dr. White was in attendance, and told me he was unconscious and more dangerously injured than his father."

Surgeon General Barnes joined the other doctors in trying to repair the mutilated and broken victims of the massacre. All of them agreed—erroneously, it turned out—that Frederick Seward would die. Augustus, Robinson, and Hansel were all weak from loss of blood, but their wounds, though gory, were without danger. Seward himself posed a bigger problem. He was recovering from a near-fatal accident when the new wounds were added. The loss of blood to such a man—aged and already injured—caused the doctors to worry. But William Seward would live, though he would never again allow a photograph to be taken of the right side of his face; and he would, moreover, bury his wife, who never recovered from the terror of that night.

There was pain and blood enough for a battery of doctors at the Seward home that evening, and Barnes found himself joining his colleagues in moving from one to another of Powell's victims, alternating surgery with providing comfort for the uninjured relatives.

BARNES, thus engaged, was hard at work when a messenger sought him out amid the gore.

"It's President Lincoln," the messenger said. "He's dying!"

CHAPTER X

"Hail to the Chief..."

OFFICER JOHN PARKER of the Metropolitan Police Force had been waiting impatiently since the play began when, finally, the coach carrying Abraham Lincoln and his party pulled to a stop in front of Ford's New Theatre. "This way to Ford's Theatre!" the barker still hyped, "Hurry in! See President Lincoln tonight!"

Parker hurried through the lobby to greet the President, and then led the party upstairs to the balcony, through its lobby and down the couple of steps along the south wall to the outer door of the Presidential Box. The hangers-on in the lobby had passed the news to the ground-floor audience when Lincoln entered, and the word had grown from a whisper to a rumble as it spread throughout the theatre. On stage, L. A. Emerson and Laura Keene ceased their performances upon hearing the audience's cue—and as Lincoln entered the outer door to the anteroom of his box all eyes were upon him.

Professor William Withers stopped the orchestra and then promptly conducted its members in playing an old Scot's war song renamed "Hail to the Chief."

The audience rose as the players signaled Lincoln's entrance, and as the President turned from the outer door to bow to his people before entering the box, they embarrassed him completely with their applause. Once inside, he seated his guests, turned the rocker to an oblique angle facing the stage, with its back to the Box Seven door, and settled into enjoying the play.

ABOUT NINE O'CLOCK John Wilkes Booth arrived on a horse—for the third time that day—at the rear of Ford's Theatre, and this time called again for Edward Spangler. When the stagehand was freed from his duties a few minutes later, he dutifully accepted the actor's command to hold the horse's reins, but promptly delegated the chore to Peanuts Burroughs.

"I heard Deboney calling to Ned (Spangler) that Booth wanted him out in the alley," Peanuts would recall. "I did not see Booth come up the alley on his horse, but I saw the horse at the door when Spangler called me out there to hold it. When Spangler told me to hold the horse I said I could not; I had to go in to attend to my door. He told me to hold it, and if there were anything wrong to lay the blame on him. So I held the horse. I held him as I was sitting over against the house there, on a carpenter's bench."

SEVERAL MINUTES LATER, Sergeant Joseph M. Dye saw "several persons, whose appearance excited my suspicions, conferring together upon the pavement," in front of Ford's.

"The first who appeared was an elegantly-dressed gentleman who came out of the passage and commenced conversing with a ruffianly looking fellow; then another appeared, and the three conversed together." The first act was almost over.

The sergeant was close enough to hear the well-dressed man say, "I think he will come out now," and as the sergeant watched, the three men positioned themselves between the theatre's front door and the President's carriage, which waited at the curb. "They watched awhile, and the rush came down," the sergeant remembered about that intermission. "Many gentlemen came out and went in and had a drink in the saloon below."

As the crowd wandered back into the theatre for the remainder of the play, Sergeant Dye saw the well-dressed man walk into the Star Saloon. Peter Taltavul, owner and bartender at the Star, recalled that Wilkes arrived around that time—"I judge a little after ten o'clock, walked up to the bar, and called for some whiskey which I gave him. He then called for some water, which I also gave him. He placed the money on the counter and went out. I saw him go out of the bar alone, as near as I can judge, from eight to ten minutes before I heard the cry that the President was assassinated."

Sergeant Dye subsequently saw the well-dressed man leave the Star and enter "the passage that leads to the stage from the street. Then the smallest one stepped up, looked at the clock in the vestibule, called the time, just as the best-dressed gentleman appeared again. Then he started up the street, remained there awhile, and came down again and called the time again. I then began to think there was something going on, and looked toward the man as he called the time. Presently he went up again, and then came down and called the time louder. I think it was ten minutes after ten that he called out the last time. He was announcing the time to the other two, and then started on a fast walk up the street, and the best-dressed one went inside the theatre." Sgt. Dye would later identify a picture of John Wilkes Booth as being that of the well-dressed man. Neither the "ruffianly looking" man nor the third man—"the one that called the time"—were ever identified.

On the stage at Ford's, Harry Hawkes, who is playing the lead part in *Our American Cousin*, Asa Trenchert, is well into his lines from Act II, Scene 3: "Keep the sun out of your eyes, look straight, pull strong, calculate the distance—and you're sure to hit the mark in most things as well as shooting."

No matter the stage, Wilkes now climbs the stairs to the balcony level and turns to walk down the rear corridor at the audience's right. He carries with him three weapons—a heavy, bone-handled bowie knife, a single-shot derringer pistol, and his own calling card.

"I was sitting in the aisle leaning by the wall toward the door of the President's Box," Captain Theodore McGowan remembered, "when a man came and disturbed me in my seat, causing me to push my chair forward to permit him to pass. He stopped about three feet from where I was sitting, and leisurely took a survey of the house. I looked at him because he happened to be in my line of sight. He took a small pack of visiting cards from his pocket, selecting one and replacing the others, stood a second perhaps, with it in his hand, and then showed it to the President's messenger, who was sitting just below him. Whether the messenger took the card into the Box or, after looking at it, allowed him to go in, I do not know; but, in a moment or two more, I saw him go through the door of the lobby leading to the Box and close the door."

DOWN UPON THE STAGE the "American cousin" is telling the gold-digging Georgina Mountchessington and her mother that he is penniless, not the heir to a fortune, as they believed him to be.

"Not heir to the fortune, Mr. Trenchert?"

"I'm offering her my heart and hand just as she wanted them; nothing in them."

"You nasty beast!" screams Georgina.

"I am aware, Mr. Trenchert," says the mother, "that you are not used to the manners of good society and that, alone, will excuse the impertinence of which you are guilty!"

Together, the two actresses stalk past Harry Hawkes and out of the wings at a point just under the President's Box, carrying the stage action to the extreme right and leaving Hawkes himself positioned below Lincoln's box, toward the rear of the stage.

The President tilts forward in his rocker, leaning over the box railing to follow the action.

"Don't know the manners of good society, eh!" says Hawkes.

And Lincoln's own laughter joins with that of the audience to cover the soft noise of the door opening slowly just behind his rocking chair.

So small is the distance between the inward-opening door and the President's rocker that, had Lincoln not leaned forward, the back of his chair would have been jarred by the motion of the slowly opening door. Wilkes has charmed his way past the outer door and locked it behind him, using the homemade wedge; now as the door swings wide, he lifts his left hand, and Harry Hawkes continues his punch line: "Waal, I guess I know enough to turn you inside-out, old gal, you sockdologizing old man trap!"

LINCOLN, perhaps hearing Booth, begins to turn his head to the left just as the pistol touches point blank behind his left ear.

PROFESSOR WILLIAM WITHERS, the orchestra leader, was returning to the pit when he heard the pistol shot. "As I turned round I heard some confusion, and I saw a man running toward me with his head down. I did not know what was the matter, and stood completely paralyzed. As he ran, I could not get out of his way, so he hit me on the leg and turned me around, and made two cuts at me, one in the neck and one on the side, and knocked me from the third entrance down to the second."

In the audience, Joseph B. Steward "heard an exclamation, and simultaneously a man leaped from the President's Box, lighting on the stage. He came down with his back slightly toward the audience, but rising and turning, his face came in full view. At the same instant I jumped on the stage, and the man disappeared at the left-hand stage entrance. I ran across the stage as quickly as possible, following the direction he took, and calling out: 'Stop that man!' "

"AT THE MOMENT the President was shot," James Ferguson remembered, "he was leaning his hand on the railing, looking down at a person in the orchestra; holding the flag that decorated the Box aside to look between it and the post. I saw the flash of the pistol right back in the Box. As the person jumped over and lit on the stage, I saw it was Booth."

THE DERRINGER is a small and inaccurate pistol except at very short range, so it needs only a small charge of powder, one that explodes with a blunt and staccato sound. The .44-caliber molded ball chosen by Wilkes Booth is one that is guaranteed to kill at short range. Fired behind Lincoln's left ear, it traversed the brain and came to rest a bit behind the right eye.

BOOTH pulled hard on the back of the President's rocking chair —flipping Lincoln's now-paralyzed body upright and to the rear—and jumped between Lincoln's knees and the box rail.

Major Henry R. Rathbone, the President's guest that night, "was intently observing the proceedings on the stage with my back toward the door" when he heard the pistol shot.

Rathbone lunged toward Booth, who "wrested himself from my grasp and made a violent thrust at my breast with a large knife. I parried the blow by striking it up, and received a wound several inches deep in my left arm, between the elbow and the shoulder." Between the two fighting men Mary Todd Lincoln was now screaming, clutching toward her husband—and the laughter of the audience was turning into a confused and frightened silence as Rathbone "endeavored to seize him . . . but only caught his clothes as he leaped over the railing of the Box."

Even given the height of the box, the jump would have been

a simple one for the athletic Booth and, with only a single actor on the stage, would have been the first step of an easy escape. But Rathbone's interference hadn't been counted into the plan, and the Union officer's grip upon the young actor's coat threw him off balance, forcing him to kick away from the box rather than to leap. The spur of Booth's right boot caught in the Treasury Guard's flag and then scratched across the carefully framed portrait of George Washington, causing Booth to land even more off stride. He hit hard and off balance, and felt pain in his lower leg as he sank down hard against it until the bone split upward against his weight. Behind him he could hear the First Lady's screams, joined by the audience's voices and the loud shrieks of Major Rathbone's fiancée.

As Booth heard the shrill cries of the audience he began to scramble across the stage, still holding the long knife to fight his way to his horse. A man from the audience began to climb over the footlights behind him, forcing Booth to torture his broken leg in a run to the stage rear—where he slashed away at former friends and colleagues, clawing his way to the open rear door.

He climbed on his horse and kicked it blindly into motion, sending Peanuts Burroughs reeling with a blow from the butt of his knife—and then, with the horse nervously moving backward and forward in an effort to obey his panicked commands, he at last moved north up the alleyway to H Street, where he turned to the right, toward the east, as the pain in his leg began driving hard up to make him ease the foot's weight against the stirrup.

Behind him, in the audience, voices began muttering: "Booth!" And in a moment a score of voices, and then a hundred began shouting, almost in a chant, "Booth! Booth! Booth!"

CHAPTER XI

"The Midnight Special"

INSIDE THE DARK and sightless hallway John Wilkes Booth holds his arms outward so that the fingertips of each hand can feel the parallel walls to guide him. At long last, after he has gone only a few feet, he can see the light filtering through the spaces between the thresholds of the two doors now before him, and through their keyholes. It has worked like a charm, so far.

The guard had read his calling card. "Yessir, Mr. Booth!" Parker had said. "No problem at all! Please go right in!"

Booth smiled, at first—then the smile faded. A national hero does not become a national villain without regret or remorse.

But he cannot pause too long. He knows Powell is now scheduled to begin the attack against Seward, but he does hesitate. There have been a couple of mistakes already, and he worries that the horse waiting for him in the alley looks too much like the one he was careful to be seen upon earlier. Not that it matters much, since he will change mounts with Herold, anyway, after crossing the bridge into Maryland.

If Herold shows up at all.

Booth shakes off the worry, reminding himself that Davie Herold isn't as dumb as he lets on—and that Herold knows his way around both Washington and Maryland. To encourage himself, the actor runs through the plan once more in his own mind.

The guard at the bridge will remember that a man named Booth crossed on a small bay horse. And a man named Smith followed on a large gray horse. They will find the evidence in Atzerodt's room in the morning. Booth regrets having to leave the Canadian bank book in the coat, but it was the most credible evidence; the map of Virginia in the pocket with it should convince everyone that his course was to the south—and then they will begin searching the peninsula for a man on a small bay. In the peninsula area, Davie Herold could escape a dozen search parties, small bay or no small bay—and if all goes well, Davie Herold will be riding the small bay all over the peninsula, leaving tracks wherever he can; he will be assisted by the numerous sympathizers who will show themselves throughout lower Maryland, looking and talking like the assassin.*

Booth's mind returns to the present. He is in the hallway, and before him are the doors to Boxes Seven and Eight. The one to his left separates him from the President of the United States. Beyond that door—and that man—is a simple jump to the stage.

But once there, he will be instantly recognized.

Once he is seen upon that stage, there is no hope for him, no way to ever again pick up the life he has known and enjoyed. Now doubt crosses his mind—the last line in the diary he will keep is a quote from Macbeth which in its entirety reads: "They have tied me to a stake—I cannot fly—but, bear-like, I must fight the course."

---

* The collusion of Southern partisans—and the human tendency to see what one expects to see—may have been behind the numerous sightings of a man on a crutch in the peninsula.

Powell is striking now, and Booth has gone too far to quit. With the thumb of his left hand he pulls the hammer of the small derringer past the first click of the safety; and then, following the second click, he eases it down against the latch so that a pull upon the trigger will unleash it. With his right hand he reaches across to the left, turns the door handle until he feels the catch release itself, and then gently shoves it swinging forward on its hinges.

"WHO ARE YOU, SIR?" the sergeant asked; and behind him was the bar blocking the rickety little bridge spanning the creek and swamp which separated Washington's Navy Yard from Maryland.

The man faced with answering that question sat upon a small bay horse, the sergeant would remember, its skin shining and its chest heaving with the air it gulped eagerly to restore the oxygen lost during a fast run. It was a restive and uneasy horse, but it bore a calm and relaxed rider.

"My name is Booth."
"Where are you coming from?"
"The city."
"Where are you going?"
"I'm going home."
"Where is your home?"
"In Charles."
"Where do you live in Charles County?"
"No town."

Sergeant Silas Cobb was standing duty, as he had done before, at one of the many exits from Washington. He had stood night duty before, and had bent the rules of curfew for errant husbands and drunken sons as well as for dutiful workers in the departments. Now, on another routine night, another apparent exception to the rule sat before him atop a horse, looked and talked relaxed, and seemed both dressed and mounted like a gentleman.

"You must live in some town," Sergeant Cobb stated.

"I live close to Beantown," came the answer, "but do not live in the town."

"Nobody's allowed to cross the bridge after nine o'clock," Sergeant Cobb answered. "Why are you out so late?"

"I didn't know about the rule; I waited for the moon to come out before riding home."

It had been a dark night, indeed. And the moon had risen just before the rider approached Sergeant Cobb's post. When asked about it later, the noncom answered honestly and simply, "I thought he was a proper person to pass and I passed him."

John Wilkes Booth, after all, was a fine actor.

David Herold, giving a false name and the excuse that he'd been carousing "in bad company," was allowed to pass approximately ten minutes later, and was a half-mile or so behind Wilkes when the actor, "riding very fast," reined up as he met a gentleman named Polk Gardiner heading in the other direction.

"Have you seen a rider going this way?" Booth asked. And when Gardiner said he had not, Booth asked the direction to Marlboro and rode off again.

Booth and Herold eventually met each other somewhere between Good Hope Hill, where Gardiner had seen them separately, and Surratt's Tavern, some ten miles farther on, where they exchanged horses.

"LLOYD?" the innkeeper recalled Herold ordering, "For God's sake, make haste and get those things."

Some six weeks earlier, Lloyd had been given two Spencer carbines by John Surratt and had kept them hidden away in an unused room until that afternoon. When Mary Surratt visited him, he said, she had given him a field glass and told him to "have the shooting-irons ready because they would be called for that evening."* Dutifully he had taken the carbines to his bedroom, and after being told that Booth could not carry a rifle, he turned over only one of the weapons and the field glass

---

* Though the rifles and the glass were given to Lloyd, there is no corroboration of Mrs. Surratt's quote. Undoubtedly she never uttered it.

Mrs. Surratt had brought that afternoon. Meanwhile, Herold had poured himself a drink, and Lloyd emerged from the house in time to see Wilkes polishing off a long draught from the bottle.

Herold gave the tavern keeper a dollar for his trouble, and then mounted the small bay horse which Booth had ridden from Washington.

"I will tell you some news," Herold yelled to Lloyd, "if you want to hear it!"

"I'm not particular," Lloyd answered. "Use your own pleasure about telling me."

"Well," Herold answered, "I am pretty certain that we have assassinated the President and Secretary Seward!"

AT THAT MOMENT John Wilkes Booth sat atop the large gray horse David Herold had ridden out of Washington. Having taken pains to be seen atop a small bay in Washington that afternoon, Booth now rode the animal which Herold had taken such pains to carefully select during that period—a strong mount capable of making a long, hard ride, and bearing no possible similarity to any descriptions the military authorities would be telegraphing to their outposts.

Up until the moment when he turned that gray horse from the yard before Surratt's Tavern, John Booth gave every indication of being a man following a carefully conceived plan of escape. Behind him, in Washington, he has left a host of clues. At least a dozen witnesses will recall seeing him upon the small bay. Sergeant Cobb—who saw him on it—even knows his name. And since he wore no disguise (such as the false beard he would later exhibit at Dr. Mudd's home) when he jumped onto the Ford's Theatre stage in prominent view of an audience who had often in the past cheered such an appearance, he could have no doubt that Cobb would quickly be given an opportunity to use such information.

The calling card he had left for Andrew Johnson could be counted on to send detectives searching through the Kirkwood

Hotel, to find—in Atzerodt's room directly above the quarters of Vice President Johnson—a bank book which identified its owner to be John Wilkes Booth and a map indicating that the assassin had been studying an escape route to the south.

The Federals would pounce upon the clues and deduce that the map was their key to the assassin's escape. Wilkes was counting upon such a determination—was, for that matter, betting his very life that they would leap at his bait and begin to search for him in the South. That was his hope for escaping to the north, to Canada—that the Federals wouldn't question the obviousness of the clues, but would instead follow them, as indeed they did.

Atzerodt's own nickname—Port Tobacco—derived from the fact that he was the primary link in any escape route to the south. It was Atzerodt's ferryboat, operating from Port Tobacco, Maryland, across the Potomac to the Virginia shore, that had transported many Confederate spies from Richmond to Washington and back again. If Booth's aim had been directed toward the south, Atzerodt would have been the conspiracy's indispensable man.

To plan an escape to the south without Atzerodt's ferryboat waiting in readiness would have been foolish; to attempt it without Atzerodt after leaving clues both blatantly and unnecessarily in his possession where they would certainly be discovered would have been idiotic. It would certainly not be in keeping with an assassin who had taken no measures to avoid being identified at the scene of the crime and who had chosen to identify himself at one point on an escape route—the Anacostia bridge—which opened only toward the south. Nor, for that matter, would it have been in keeping with a man who had laid his plans with sufficient care to rendezvous with a co-conspirator at a location where they had previously secreted additional arms.

LESS THAN FORTY MILES from Surratt's Tavern is the primary northbound railroad station in Baltimore, Maryland. Leaving

Surratt's Tavern at midnight atop a succession of strong horses, a skilled rider could rendezvous with the train inside of those necessary nine hours—though his mounts might die as a result.*

JOHN BOOTH had been a skilled rider since his teens. He could have made the train. If he had done so, he would be moving northward at the same time that his pursuers began looking for him on the Maryland Peninsula.

That train would arrive in New York City at 5:37 P.M. on Saturday, April 15, 1865. Hours later, at 12:15 in the afternoon, another train would pull out of the Manhattan Station; it would move northward into New York State, and then east into Connecticut before turning again north to follow the Connecticut River Valley up into Vermont. It was called "The Midnight Special," and after stopping in St. Albans, Vermont, it would cross the border into Canada and complete its run at the main station in Montreal.

John Harrison Surratt, Jr., admitted later to being in St. Albans, having "provided myself with an oxford-cut jacket and round-top hat peculiar to Canada at that time," on the very day that train arrived.

John Surratt never explained his dalliance in St. Albans, even while admitting that he had taken the precaution of disguising himself. By the eighteenth, the heat was being felt even in St. Albans, and after a close brush with a detective, Surratt at last took the evening train across the border and immediately went into hiding.

BUT WHEN BOOTH AND HEROLD turned their horses away from the front of Surratt's Tavern, neither man turned north toward Baltimore. Instead, they headed south toward the little town called T.B.

It is six miles from Surrattsville to T.B., and eleven miles

---

* Union armies surrounded Washington. North of them were two boarding points for Booth—Baltimore and Annapolis Junction. Either could have been reached on the assassination night by horse.

farther south is the little farm where they stopped—a farm owned by Dr. Samuel A. Mudd. It was the first way station on what was to become their aimless and wandering suicide—Wilkes' broken leg was far too painful for any other course.

No matter how carefully the plan was laid, it could not have included fixing the assassin's broken leg.

THAT IS, in fact, where everything went wrong. It was that simple. Wilkes meant to go north, but because of the leg had to go south. That unplanned-for broken leg explains why George Atzerodt—whose ferryboat was the traditional way to Richmond—was in Washington the night of the murder instead of standing by his boat at Port Tobacco. It explains Booth's meaning when he wrote in his diary that "I have a greater desire and almost a mind to return to Washington and, in a measure, clear my name, which I feel I can do."

It explains why Booth gave his real name to Sergeant Cobb at the Anacostia bridge, and Herold did not.

It explains all the concern about renting horses the day of the assassination; it explains all the evidence left behind in Atzerodt's room at the Kirkwood—not to mention Booth's calling card left behind for Andrew Johnson or his secretary to find and turn over to the authorities.

Most importantly, it explains why John Wilkes Booth—who moved with much certainty from Ford's New Theatre to Surratt's Tavern—spent the rest of his life in aimless and hopeless wanderings down the Maryland Peninsula, across the Potomac, and into an accidental meeting with men who called themselves Confederate guerrillas just a few miles from Richard Garrett's small Virginia farmhouse.

HE WASN'T going south at all. That is the explanation. All of his machinations, all of his deceptions, all of his efforts to point the authorities at George Atzerodt were meant to lead the soldiers and detectives in massive numbers into the south.

But then his leg and his plans were broken.

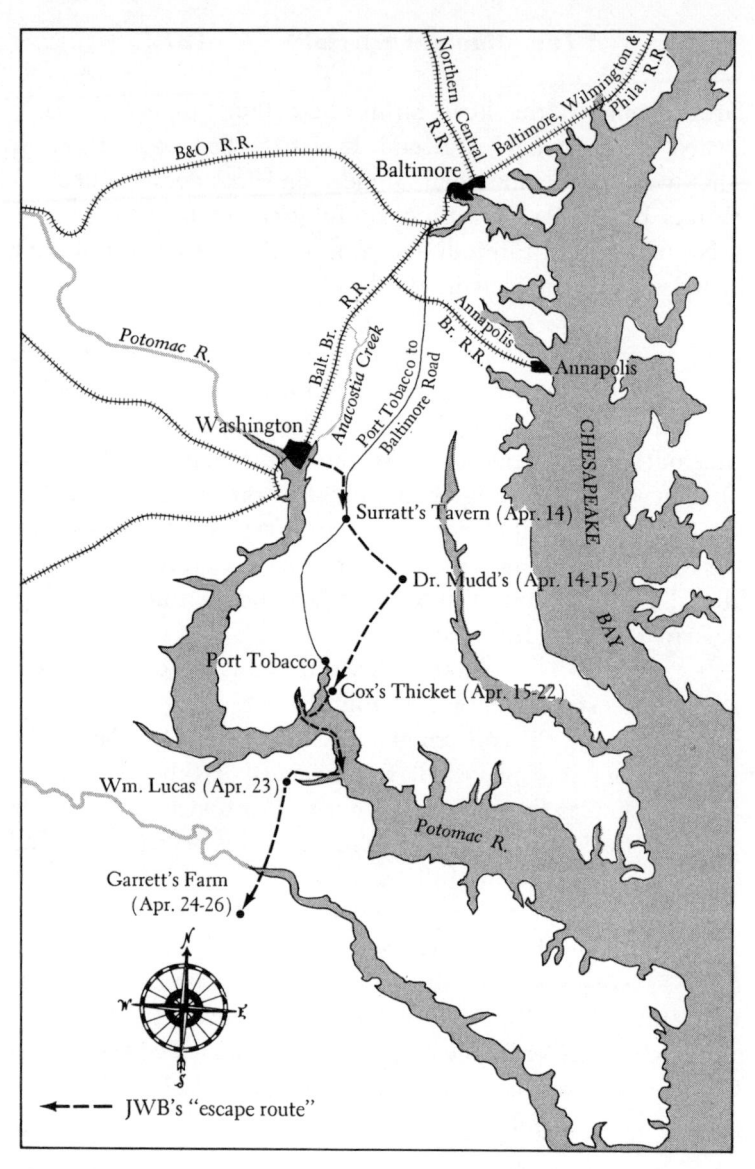

John Wilkes Booth's "escape route"—in actuality it is one day of flight followed by a week of hiding in a damp and cold thicket, then another day of flight followed by two days of hiding in disguise at Garrett's farm. There is no evidence of advance planning for any of his stopovers except the first, at Surratt's Tavern.

CHAPTER XII

Running Away on One Leg

IT WAS WELL PAST the middle of the night when Dr. Samuel Mudd was aroused from sleep by a persistent fist hammering on his door.

He could hardly be expected to recognize either Herold—who stood upon his doorstep—or Booth—who sagged, exhausted, on his mount a few yards away—in the overcast blackness of the moonless night.* Mudd recalled later, under oath, that Davie Herold told him they were travelers who had

---

* Dr. Mudd steadfastly denied that he recognized Booth during the assassin's visit. He was, it must be remembered, trying to save himself from the hangman when he did so. Furthermore, there are too many indications that he knew Booth well to permit belief that the doctor suspected neither the identity of his patient nor the fact that he was a fugitive from some crime. For his own part, Booth—not knowing how trustworthy Mudd would be when he learned the exact nature of the crime, and worried enough about whether the broken leg would cause him to be caught—would understandably attempt to hide his identity. What is most likely is

been diverted from their trip to Washington when his friend's horse fell, causing the fellow to injure his leg.

Dr. Mudd helped Booth from his horse and into the parlor of his home, where the actor collapsed on a sofa. "After getting a light," Mudd recounted later, "I assisted him in getting upstairs where there were two beds, one of which he took. He seemed to be very much injured in the back, and complained very much of it. I did not see his face at all. He seemed to be tremulous and not inclined to talk, and had his cloak thrown around his head and seemed inclined to sleep, as I thought, in order to ease himself; and every now and then he would groan pretty heavily."

Between his groans, Booth urged the doctor to hurry. Mudd found the swelling in the leg necessitated cutting the assassin's boot away, and used a knife to split the leather "longitudinally, in front of the instep."

After removing the boot and absent-mindedly tossing it into a corner, Mudd found "a straight fracture of the tibia about two inches above the ankle. My examination was quite short, and I did not find the adjoining bone fractured in any way. I do not suppose I was more than three-quarters of an hour in making the examination of the wound and applying the splint. He continued still to suffer and complained of severe pain in the back, especially when being moved. In my opinion, pain in the back may arise from riding. I judged that in this case it originated from his fall and also from riding, as he seemed to be prostrated. He sometimes breathed very shortly and as if exhausted."

The examination had worn out the night. Leaving his patient to rest, Mudd invited Davie Herold to join him for breakfast. Later Herold borrowed a razor for Booth, and while the actor shaved off his mustache, Mudd rigged up a pair of crutches. The actor, according to Mudd's wife, continued to wear an ill-

---

that the doctor did not ask for, nor did Booth volunteer, any information regarding the actor's identity or why he was choosing to hide it. Thus Mudd's story is *technically* true.

fitting stage beard,* which from time to time fell loose from his chin.

Booth was forcing a consciousness bent on survival into conflict with his own complete exhaustion. But some time during that morning he succumbed to sleep.

Davie Herold ate lunch alone with Dr. Mudd, and afterwards —while Booth slept—Herold rode with Mudd, as the doctor would later recall, "over to my father's place in order to see if we could get a carriage for the wounded man; but I found that the carriages were all out of repair except for one, and we could not get that one." Mudd then left for Briantown to borrow a conveyance to get Booth and Herold away. ". . . I then went down to Mr. Hardy's and was in conversation with him fully an hour when I returned home leisurely and found the two men were just in the act of leaving."

On the outskirts of Briantown—only four miles south of Mudd's home—Herold had found Union soldiers instead of the carriage he had gone to seek, and sped in panic back to Booth. After rousing Booth and asking Mudd for directions, Davie Herold fled with his leader into the Zekiah Swamps.

About nine o'clock that night their paths crossed that of Oscar Swann, a black man, from whom they demanded—upon the threat of death—directions to the plantation of Colonel Samuel Cox. "When they got to Cox's they got off," Swann remembered. "It was near midnight. Cox came out with a candle."

Herold warned Swann to wait for them in silence: "Don't you say anything. If you tell that you saw anybody, you will not live long."

The colonel said, "How do you do?" to the fugitives and invited them inside.

Three or four hours later, only a while before Easter Sunday's sunrise, Booth and Herold, both thoroughly disgruntled,

* Which of course raises the question of why he did not use the beard to disguise himself at Ford's Theatre.

emerged from the mansion house—named "Rich Hill." Booth barked at Herold to help him mount his horse, and Swann was once again pressed into service to assist.

"I thought Cox was a man of Southern feeling." Swann heard one of the two men say. Then they paid him twelve dollars and dismissed him. Judging from Cox's subsequent assistance, it appears the actor was putting on a performance solely for Swann's benefit.

COX'S STEPBROTHER, Thomas A. Jones, lived nearby at a less sumptuous farm which he had named "Huckleberry." On Easter Sunday morning the colonel's son called on his step-uncle with a message to drop by as soon as possible to discuss some seed corn. "I knew that was not the real cause for his sending for me, but I saddled my horse at once and went with the boy," Jones later recalled.

Colonel Cox met Thomas Jones at the front gate of Rich Hill, and walked with him quite a distance from the house before speaking. "There were two men called at my house this morning before daybreak," the colonel said, "and I think one was Booth. Now, we want you to take charge of them, feed and care for them, and get them across the river as soon as you can. We must help them as they are on our side."

"I'll see what I can do," Jones answered, "but I must see these men first. Where are they?"

Cox answered that his overseer, Franklin Robey, who was an acquaintance of Herold's, had taken both men to a thick section of the pine woods, hidden them and warned them to remain silent.

Jones, a Rebel agent himself, found the hiding place with no difficulty since it was near a tree stump the Confederates used as a letter drop. "As I drew near the hiding place of the fugitives," Jones remembered, "I stopped and gave the signal" that Cox had described to him—a peculiar whistle.

After a short delay, Herold emerged from the thicket. "Who are you," he wanted to know, "and what do you want?"

"I come from Cox. I'm a friend. You have nothing to fear."

Herold lowered his carbine and led Jones through the underbrush to the fugitives' campsite. There, for the first time, Jones saw John Booth. He was "lying on the wet, cold ground, his head supported by his hand. His weapons of defense were close beside him; an old blanket was partly drawn over him. His slouch hat and crutch were lying by him; he was exceedingly pale, and his features bore traces of intense suffering. . . . Murderer though I knew him to be . . . I determined to do all I could to get him into Virginia, and so assured him."

Booth held out his hand to Jones and thanked him. "I killed President Lincoln," he said, "and knew the United States Government would use every means in its power to capture me. But John Wilkes Booth will never be taken alive."

FOR THE NEXT FIVE DAYS Thomas Jones visited the fugitives daily, bringing them food, liquor and newspapers. In the meantime, he had a boat hidden away for them near the river, in Dent's Meadow, and on one occasion visited Port Tobacco. There he tried to snoop out information that would be useful to Booth—information which would aid him in escaping across the Potomac into Virginia.

Federal gunboats were now fully alerted to watch for the fugitives, and Port Tobacco—as the regular embarkation and debarkation point for Confederate spies traveling between Virginia and northern points—provided the best access to information about the scheduling of the gunboat patrols and the numbers of boats.

Booth's thoughts must have occasionally wandered to the subject of George Atzerodt—so carefully set up to draw attention toward a flight into Virginia, and now so perfectly set up to deny Booth himself an easy escape. Wilkes Booth also read the newspapers Jones brought to him daily. His own name came up for the first time in the April 16 edition of the *National Intelligencer*:

"John Wilkes Booth, who was convicted by the public sentiment as the assassin of the President, is a son of the great deceased tragedian Lucius Brutus Booth [sic] and a brother of the eminent actor, Edwin Booth. It is a strange thing if he be guilty of this crime. He is a young fellow of spirit, of acute mind, and of great professional vigor, whose thoughts have lately been turned away from the stage, of which he was an ornament."

The praises stand in stark contrast to the editorial eulogy of Lincoln that appeared on the same page, its writer obviously having a hard time finding nice things to say about the departed: "His conduct of the war is generally conceded to have been all that could have been expected of a statesman of limited experience. . . . His was not a remote and dazzling character, admired and followed like that of a Napoleon, or of a Clay, or a Jackson: but it was rather that of an honest neighbor or relative. . . . while his friends supposed that there were many more brilliant and perhaps more able men, they felt that none was so safe as he. . . ."

Noting that Booth was rumored to have made sixty thousand dollars in oil speculations, the author of the story in the *Intelligencer* followed his praises of Booth's professional skills with the first hint of what would generally be accepted for a century as the reason for the murder: "His temper is romantic and poetical, his disposition has been considered as gentle. There were no circumstances nor antecedents (independently or thus far disclosed) to mark him as a man likely to conceive or to execute such a crime." But, the reporter continued, "there is a singular history to this Booth family, the half of which we have neither time nor space to detail. . . . [The father, Junius Brutus Booth] was ever marked by eccentricities which made him liable to be called insane, as in fact he often was, certainly from the effect of drink, if not constitutionally."

Another point is then made—a point the significance of which was overlooked for a century: "When he committed this act, if he did commit it, he must have been aware that he would be recognized generally by the audience, and especially by Miss Laura Keene and some of her troupe who were engaged in the play on that fatal night, to whom he was particularly well known personally. He seems to have taken no precaution in the way of disguise."

The editorial comments quoted above were run apart from the basic news story naming the assassin, an indication of the haste and confusion with which everyone from the War Department to the busy *Intelligencer* reporters and typographers were trying to separate rumor from fact.

"Developments," the news story read, "have rendered it certain that the hand which deprived our President of life was that of John Wilkes Booth, an actor. Since his arrival in the city he is said to have declared that he traveled three days and three nights in order to reach here in time. His identification as the man who leaped from the Box is complete. . . ."

In yet another column was more alleged information: "Boston, April 15 — This forenoon a gentleman stated in Barton's Saloon, No. 41 Congress Street, that he had been told by J. Wilkes Booth within a few weeks, that he intended to kill President Lincoln. . . . His name is J. H. Borland, and he belongs to Pittsburgh, Pa. . . ."*

In a subsequent dispatch from Boston, it is said of Booth that "when he left this city he expressed his undying hatred of the North and of the Union, and threw out some vague hints of vengeance which were not regarded at the time as meaning any more than that the rebellion should succeed."

---

* The quote is reproduced here to demonstrate the kind of rumor prevalent in the early reports. No further reference to Mr. Borland can be found.

Booth was probably disappointed at not finding reprinted in the *Intelligencer* the letter he had left Friday afternoon with John Matthews—with instructions that Matthews give it to the newspaper's editors on the next day. Or he may have paid special attention to the conclusion drawn by those same editors: "His statements, if arrested, would be of the greatest interest, and we believe they would be a frank revelation of all that he knows in the matter. If he be the source of this tragedy, what were his motives, what the inducement to such a man? These are peculiarly interesting questions as applied to his case."

JOHN WILKES BOOTH, camping in the springtime chills of the Maryland swamp country, carried with him a red leather wallet that he had evidently bought during 1864, since its contents included a "pocket secretary" type of calendar for that year. The pages before those of June 1864 are missing, either because he used them for memoranda or because someone in the War Department destroyed them after his death; but on the first of the remaining pages is a statement composed in that Maryland pine thicket, with Booth no doubt resting his back against the tree where Thomas Jones first saw him, and writing in a small and unflourished script, trying to back-date his account while giving away the ruse in the text:

> April 14, Friday, the Ides. Until today nothing was ever thought of sacrificing to our country's wrongs. For six months we had worked to capture. But, our cause being almost lost, something decisive and great must be done. But its failure was owing to others who did not strike for their country with a heart. I struck boldly and not as the papers say. I walked with a firm step through a thousand of his friends, was stopped, but pushed on. A Colonel was at his side. I shouted "Sic semper" before I fired. In jumping broke my leg. I passed all his pickets, rode sixty miles that night with the bone of my leg tearing the flesh at every jump. I can never repent it. Though we hated to kill. Our country owed all her trouble to him, and God simply made

me the instrument of his punishment. The country is not what it was. This forced Union is not what I have loved. I care not for what becomes of me. I have no desire to outlive my country. This night before the deed, I wrote a long article and left it for one of the editors of "The National Intelligencer," in which I fully set forth our reasons for our proceedings.

On subsequent days, Jones brought other newspapers—and Booth may have written in response to them as well, but there are more missing pages which from the rip marks appear to have been removed in a bunch* rather than one at a time.

THE NEXT ENTRY is dated April 21. Probably written in the early morning hours of April 22, it tells of a wearing and debilitating night on the river.

Thomas Jones remembered later that on "Friday evening, April 21, the opportune time seemed to have presented itself" to try crossing the Potomac into Virginia.

Booth began to shiver as the threesome moved from the thicket toward the concealed boat. There is little question that he was in agony from exposure and the now-swelling break in his leg. Jones, however, turned aside any suggestion of stopping over in Huckleberry. Only a day or so earlier, Jones himself had turned down a detective's offer of one hundred thousand dollars for information about Booth, and he was reluctant to chance having a spy see the now-known cripple.

The three men "went to the house and took what I thought would be enough for two men and carried it out to them. . . . After supper we resumed our journey across the open field for the longed-for river. When about three hundred yards from the

---

* It is generally believed that Booth's diary fell into Stanton's hands after his death. For unknown reasons, possibly evidence showing the innocence of Mrs. Surratt, a large chunk of pages, apparently torn out together, was destroyed when the diary eventually materialized from the archives of the War Department.

river, Herold and myself assisted Booth to dismount.* The path was steep and narrow, and for three men to walk down it abreast was not the least difficult part of that night's work. At length we reached the shore and found the boat. It was a flat-bottomed one, about twelve feet long, of a dark lead color."

"We placed Booth in the stern with an oar to steer," Jones recounted years later, "Herold taking the bow seat to row. The night was ink-black. We could not see either of the men, and had to feel for them, and as I was in the act of pushing the boat off Booth said, 'Wait a minute, old fellow.' He then offered me some money. I took seventeen dollars, the price of the boat. In a voice choked with emotion he said, 'God bless you, my dear friend, for all you have done for me. Good-bye! Good-bye!'

"I pushed the boat off, and it glided out in the darkness. I could see nothing, and the only sound was the swish of the waves. . . . I stood on the shore and listened 'til the sound of the oars died away in the distance, then climbed the hill and took my way home, and my sleep was more quiet and peaceful than it had been for sometime."

OUT ON THE RIVER, Booth and Herold either lost their way or were diverted by a federal gunboat. Instead of going to the southeast, to land on the Virginia bank, they pulled ashore northwest, up Nanjemoy Creek, to a landing place near George Atzerodt's old stomping grounds at Port Tobacco. Herold has described their reception: "We got along the Maryland shore to Nanjemoy Creek, and went to a man's house and wanted to buy some bread. He said he hadn't any baked, and would not bake any. He said he had nothing to drink, either. I said we were wet, and would like to have something to drink. I had a bottle, and asked if he would sell me some whiskey. He said he would not do it. Booth gave the man's little boy a quarter of a dollar for filling the bottle with milk."

---

* An indication of Booth's condition is the need for a horse, since Herold had shot the two mounts they had ridden to Cox's door.

Those were the circumstances upon which John Wilkes Booth made his second entry in the diary. Hidden away on the miserable early morning of April 22, he began writing:

> Friday, 21. After being hunted like a dog through swamps, woods, and last night being chased by gunboats 'til I was forced to return, wet, cold, and starving, with every man's hand against me, I am here in despair. And why? For doing what Brutus was honored for—what made Tell a Hero. And yet I, for striking down a greater tyrant than they ever knew, am looked upon as a common cut-throat. My act was purer than either of theirs. One hoped to be great himself, the other had not only his country's but his own wrongs to avenge. I hoped for no gains, I knew no private wrong. I struck for my country and that alone. A country groaned beneath this tyranny and prayed for this end, and yet now behold the cold hand they extend to me. God cannot pardon me if I have done wrong. Yet I cannot see any wrong except in serving a degenerate people. The little, the very little I left behind to clear my name the Government will not allow to be printed. So ends all. For my country I have given up all that makes life sweet and holy, brought misery upon my family, and am sure there is no pardon in the heavens for me since man condemns me so. I have only heard of what has been done (except for what I did myself) and it fills me with horror. God! Try and forgive me and Bless my Mother. Tonight I will once more try the river with the intention to cross, though I have a greater desire and almost a mind to return to Washington and in a measure clear my name which I feel I can do. I do not repent the blow I struck. I may before my God, but not to man. I think I have done well, though I am abandoned with the curse of Cain upon me, when if the world knew my heart, that one blow would have made me great, though I did desire no greatness.
> Tonight I try to escape these bloodhounds once more. Who, who reads his fate? God's will be done.
> I have too great a soul to die like a criminal. Oh, may He spare me that, and let me die bravely!
> I bless the entire world. I have never hated or wronged anyone. This last was not a wrong, unless God deems it so. And its for Him to damn or bless me.

And for this brave boy with me, who often prays (yes, before and since) with a true and sincere heart, was it crime in him. If so, why can he pray the same? I do not wish to shed a drop of blood, but "I must fight the course."* 'Tis all that's left me.

THE TWO FUGITIVES pulled out of Nanjemoy Creek without food, water or whiskey—and somehow made their way past the Union gunboats on the Potomac. They beached their little skiff in Gambo Creek, on the Virginia shore, and late in the morning Davie Herold hunted up Mrs. Emma Quesenberry at her home near the mouth of Machadoc Creek. Through her, they were put in touch with a guide named either Bryan or Bryant, who took the two men to the home of Dr. Richard H. Stewart, which was located a half-mile or so from the public road to Port Conway. There, they begged fruitlessly for help.

"I was suspicious of the urgency of the lame man," Stewart later testified. "He desired to tell something I did not care to hear. I did not really believe he had a broken leg; I thought it was all put on, although he was on two crutches. He said he had had a fall and broken his leg; he said Dr. Mudd had set it.

"The small man had a short carbine, and he had on a satchel. I did not see any arms on them; he had a large shawl around him. They were mounted on Bryant's horses...."

After being turned away from the Stewart home, Booth struck back, ripping a page from the red leather diary and commanding a black man—William Lucas—to deliver it on the following day:

"Next Monday evening," Stewart would remember, "Lucas brought a note over to my house signed 'Stranger,' with two-and-one-half dollars rolled up in it, and gave it to my wife. I was not at home. I told her that the man who wrote the note

---

* Booth's quoted line is from Macbeth. In its entirety it reads: "They have tied me to a stake. I cannot fly, but, bear-like, I must fight the course."

had given him the note to deliver to me. It was sealed. It was a leaf of a memorandum book rolled around and the money rolled up in it...."

The note from Booth to Dr. Stewart was written on one of the diary's pages. A large chunk of the paper is missing after the first three letters of the word "Dear"—which may have been torn out by Booth, by the doctor himself or by his wife to disguise him as its recipient (which may be a clue to the doctor's meaning when he said Booth "wanted to tell something I did not want to hear")—but the body of the note is intact:

> Forgive me, but I have some little pride. I cannot blame you for want of hospitality; you know your own affairs. I was sick, tired, with a broken limb, and in need of medical assistance. I would not have turned a dog away from my door in such a plight. However, you were kind enough to give us something to eat, for which I not only thank you but, on account of the reluctant manner in which it was bestowed, I feel bound to pay for it. It is not the substance, but the way in which kindness is extended that makes one happy in the acceptance thereof. The sauce to meat is ceremony; meeting were bare without it. Be kind enough to accept the enclosed five dollars,* although hard to spare, for what we have had.

The note was undoubtedly written in the tumble-down cabin of William Lucas, and if it seems bitter—and if John Wilkes Booth seems overly trod upon—consider the scene from William Lucas' point of view: "My dogs were barking and woke me up. I heard a horse and thought there might be someone trying to steal my horses. A strange voice called me.... I would not open the door, but asked who it was.... I was frightened at the time. People had been shot in that way, and I was afraid to come out."

One of the men outside mentioned Bryant's name and Lucas went outdoors.

---

* Booth and Stewart's memoirs of the sum differ.

"We want to stay here tonight," one of the men said.

"You cannot do it," Lucas answered. "I am a colored man and have no right to take care of white people. I have only one room in the house, and my wife is sick."

The first man—apparently Herold—said, "We are Confederate soldiers; we have been in service three years; we have been knocking about all night, and don't intend to any longer; but we are going to stay."

Booth, meanwhile, had apparently dismounted and walked into the house.

"Gentlemen," Lucas pleaded, "You have treated me very badly."

Booth drew a bowie knife. "Old man," he said, "how do you like that?"

"I do not like that at all," Lucas answered honestly. "I was always afraid of a knife."

"We were sent here, old man," Booth said. "We understood you have good teams."

Lucas answered that his hired hands were coming next morning to take the team for planting corn.

"Well, Dave," Booth said, "we will not go on any further, but stay here and make this old man get us his horse in the morning."

In the morning, the fugitives forced Lucas to rent them his team, but paid him in advance for it, and sent him off with the note for Stewart.

Booth and Herold arrived about noontime at the little ferryboat across the Rappahannock, which was the principal industry of Port Conway, Virginia.

"While waiting for a ferryboat," Herold remembered later, "three Confederate soldiers came along. We asked whose command they belonged to. One said to the Ninth Virginia; the other two said they belonged to Mosby's Command. They stated they were going to Bowling Green. We wanted a man who lives at Port Conway to carry us to Milford. He said he could not start until sundown. We didn't want to travel at night, having lost much rest. The three Confederate soldiers, Booth and myself—five of us—crossed the ferry from Port Conway to Port Royal.

"We tried to get a conveyance at Port Royal to take us to Milford. While I was trying to get a conveyance, Booth was talking to this man, Captain Jett. When I came back he said to Booth, 'As long as you are a Virginian and wounded, I will carry you up the country, where you can stay.'"

In this statement, Herold is fogging things quite a bit. In the first place, Davie Herold—who Powell called "Blab"—had blabbed to Jett exactly who his friend was and what both of them had done. The three Confederate "soldiers" were Mortimer B. Ruggles and A. S. Bainbridge, who are listed in records as privates in the C.S.A., and Willie S. Jett, for whom there are no service records. All were in their late teens or early twenties.

Years later, Bainbridge would say, "When Booth realized that we were kindly disposed, he threw off all reserve and became quite communicative," and Ruggles recalled that Booth confided that neither Herold nor Atzerodt knew anything of the "plot to kill."

Jett spoke little, and remains mysterious.

With Jett in the lead, the new friends of Booth and Herold led the fugitives to a home Jett highly recommended, run by the Misses Sarah Jane and Lucy Peyton. While the ladies allowed Booth to rest upon the sofa, they quickly begged their guests' pardon, explaining that Mr. Randolph Peyton was out of town and the gentlemen visitors therefore could not possibly stay overnight. The ladies suggested that perhaps Mr. Richard Garrett, who lived nearby, might be able to accommodate them.

IT WAS FOUR O'CLOCK in the afternoon when the fugitives arrived at Garrett's farm. The Virginia countryside around that farm site is hilly, and the house itself sits atop a long hill, with a gradual drop to the west, and relatively flat land to the east. Goldenvale Creek and Mill Creek flank the hill's crest.

At this time the Garretts had a guest, Mrs. Garrett's sister, L. K. B. Holloway, a one-time schoolteacher, who wrote down her recollection of Booth's arrival: "On arriving, they were met by Mr. Richard H. Garrett, who was the owner of the house, upon which Jett addressed him, 'This is Mr. Garrett, I presume?' And on securing an affirmative answer, introduced to him the second unknown as his friend, John William Boyd, 'a Confederate soldier who has been wounded in the battles around Richmond, near Petersburg.' At the same time he requested Mr. Garrett to take care of him until Wednesday morning, at which time he would call for him. Complying with this request, Mr. Garrett consented to receive him."

Jett and Herold left Booth at Garrett's farm and continued on to Bowling Green, where they visited whorehouses. On the morning of April 25 they regrouped, after Herold bought a pair of shoes, and returned to the Garretts'. Jett—if he was of a mind to do it—had every opportunity to send a telegraph during this interval.

Booth's old charm had returned with a good night's sleep, and by the time the others returned he was rapidly endearing himself to the Garrett household. The assassin spent his first pleasant afternoon since April 14 sunning himself under a locust tree in the Garrett yard and, to a degree, charming Miss Holloway.

Less than five miles away federal troops were closing the gap.

Jett returned that night to Bowling Green, and controversy surrounds his actions.

While he was gone, Booth entertained the Garretts' sons by shooting at and missing a knothole in the gatepost, owing to a "sluggish" trigger on the old revolver they had given him.

That night the federal soldiers and Jett came together, and

whether the meeting was upon their—or his—initiative, Jett led them to the Garrett home.

THE LAZY, COMFORTABLE AFTERNOON had ended early for Booth. One of the Garrett sons had learned the Federals were looking for a man on crutches traveling with a friend, and his suspicions were confirmed when at the passage of a Union patrol, both Booth and Herold lit out for the woods. "If you've gotten into any difficulty, you must leave at once," the boy told Booth. "I don't want you to bring any trouble upon my aged father."

Booth assured Bill Garrett that the trouble was over, but seemed too eager to hire a horse to get away.

"When the hour came to retire," Miss Holloway remembered, "Boyd (Booth) saw no place in which he could be made comfortable. He said that anywhere would do rather than go upstairs.

"Then he and Herold were conducted to a large tobacco house in which was stored a lot of valuable furniture belonging to the people of Port Royal, covered with hay and other provender.

"After they entered, Jack Garrett locked the door and took the key to the house and gave it to me, saying he would leave it in my care and that I must not let anyone have it, as it was his opinion that they intended to steal their horses and escape. Then, assuring themselves, he and his brother . . . went out into a shed opposite the tobacco house to spend the night. . . ."

ABOUT TWO O'CLOCK in the morning federal troops surrounded the Garrett farm.

When every man was in position, an officer began banging on the door, demanding entrance, and when Richard Garrett, still in his night dress, opened the door, he was dragged outside. Uncooperative when the officers asked him about his guests, he was ordered to a locust tree where a noose was fastened about his throat. Garrett saw Jett and found his tongue: "You have done this, Willie! You brought these Federals here!"

"Never mind who brought us here!" Lieutenant Baker answered immediately. "You've got one more chance, you old fool! Talk, or be hanged! Where's the two assassins?"

Five troopers caught the free end of the rope as it was thrown over the tree's limb, and then Matt Garrett stepped forward. "Gentlemen," he said, "if you want to know where those men are, I will take you to the place."

THE EXCHANGE OF KNOWLEDGE takes only an instant, and the deployment of troops only a minute.

A tobacco barn is not a solid structure: its sides are made up of widely spaced boards which permit the drying of the crop. Inside it, Booth and Herold lie low and silent as the troopers surround them.

One of the Garrett boys is sent to open the padlock on the door; fearing that he will be shot, he then comes running back. Lieutenant Baker yells to the fugitives to surrender themselves, and one of them asks for time to consider it.

Booth and the Federals apparently share the notion that Booth might believe them to be Confederate troops, and while the Federals refuse to identify themselves, hoping he will think them to be friendly Confederates and therefore come out to greet them, Booth refuses to move. At last he suggests they withdraw a hundred yards and he will come out shooting to stand against them all. When the troops refuse, he responds with the suggestion that the distance be reduced to fifty yards.

That proposition also having been rejected, Booth answered: "Well, my brave boys, prepare a stretcher for me."

One of the Garrett boys is forced to gather brush and set it against the barn wall. After a while, Booth yells out to the boy that he will be shot if he continues. Meanwhile, Davie Herold is losing his nerve.

"There's a man in here wants out," Booth yells.

Running Away on One Leg / 147

"Very well," Baker answers. "Let him hand his arms out, and come out."

Booth and Herold have obviously been arguing inside the barn, and finally Booth can be heard saying, "You damned coward, will you leave me now! Go! Go! I would not have you stay with me!"

The Federals next heard a banging from the inside and David Herold saying, "Let me out!"

"Hand out your arms," Baker demands.

"I have none."

"You carried a carbine, and you must hand it out."

"The arms are mine," John Booth answers for Herold from deep inside the barn. "And I have got them."

"This man carried a carbine," Baker argues, "and he must hand it out!"

"Upon the word and honor of a gentleman, he has no arms," Booth answers. "The arms are mine, and I have got them."

Conger whispers to Baker: "Never mind the arms; if we can get one of the men out, let us do it and wait no longer."

Herold sticks his wrists out the barn door and Baker quickly yanks him out the rest of the way, whipping him by the arms into the hands of the troopers. Meanwhile, Conger has set a match to the kindling at the rear of the barn.

Inside the barn John Wilkes Booth sees the flames begin to lick upward along the planks of the sides. He drops the carbine and picks up a Colt revolver. In the middle of the burning building he lets the crutch under his right arm fall away as he leans to the left to lift the heavy barreled weapon to his own temple. The muzzle drops, pulled by his own action as he squeezes the trigger back, and the bullet explodes into his spine instead of his brain.*

---

* A sergeant named Boston Corbett claimed that he actually shot Booth, and his story has generally been accepted. Corbett, however, was an unstable personality who had castrated himself after being tempted by a

CONGER AND BAKER hear the shot and rush inside the building. Leaning over the body, each accuses the other of killing the assassin, and then they order Booth carried from the burning shed to the grass.

His spine shattered midway down the neck, John Wilkes Booth is now little more than a conscious dead man. Conger sees Booth's eyes move and calls at once for water, which he touches to Booth's face. Booth is trying to speak, and Conger tilts his ear almost to the assassin's lips to hear him say, "Tell Mother I die for my country."

"Is that what you say?" Conger asked, and repeats the line.

"Yes," Booth whispers.

The troopers are ordered to carry him to the porch of the farmhouse, where he is laid on something resembling a straw mattress. Still speaking in a whisper, Wilkes asks for water, which is given to him. He then asks to be turned on his face.

"You cannot lie on your face," Conger answers. Then Booth asks to be turned on his side, and several times the troopers comply with his wishes, though it never relieves his pain.

At last, Booth asks Conger to press down hard upon his throat, evidently trying to cough. But though the captain cooperates, the paralysis is complete.

"Open your mouth and put out your tongue," Conger offers, "and I will see if it bleeds."

Conger tells Booth there is no blood showing.

"Kill me, kill me," Booth begs.

As the sun rises on the morning of April 26, 1865, John

---

prostitute and who later went berserk while serving as a guard at the Kansas state legislature and fired his pistol into the assembled lawmakers during a session. He was, furthermore, armed with a rifle rather than a pistol and claimed to have fired from a kneeling position. Many portions of his story jibe with neither the nature of Booth's wound nor with its trajectory. This author's own experiments with a Navy Colt similar to the one Booth carried—and which witnesses saw him raise prior to the gunshot —have led to a conviction that the actor took his own life.

Wilkes Booth asks to have his paralyzed hands raised before his eyes. "Useless, useless," he says to nobody in particular. And then, quietly and calmly, he dies.

HIS CORPSE was sewn inside a blanket and thrown into the back of a wagon for the journey to Washington. Some of the blood slopped onto an old black man's hands, and in a pitiful parody of Macbeth, the old man backed away from the reality of the corpse, wringing his hands and proclaiming that the blood stains upon them would never go away.

IN SEARCHING THE BODY, the soldiers had found the diary, some ammunition, a file, a pipe—and a Canadian bill of exchange.

CHAPTER

XIII

The Missing Link

IN 1861, due to the threat of assassination, President-elect Abraham Lincoln had traveled to Washington unheralded and incognito aboard a secret train. Just four short years later, a train would take him out again.

As the sun glistened off humming telegraph wires the morning of April 15, 1865, it cast shadows into the newly completed interior of Lincoln's official railroad car, which was sitting in the yards of the U.S. Military Railroad awaiting his first inspection. Its sixteen wheels—double the normal number—were required to support the weight of steel shielding used to protect him from harm, but he would not need such protection on his only ride aboard it.

Already in the early hours of that first morning the police had been pounding upon the door of Mrs. Mary Surratt's boarding house in Washington, looking for her twenty-three-year-old son John. But the young dispatch carrier for the Confederacy was already on his way to Canada, so the police contented themselves with taking Louis Weichmann, the border and friend of John Surratt's, into "protective custody."

At Dr. Samuel A. Mudd's home that morning, John Wilkes Booth writhed in pain as his fractured leg was placed in splints, and during Sunday, the 16th, as the body of Abraham Lincoln went under the autopsy knife, his murderer was encamped beside the Potomac in the marshy wilderness of the Maryland Peninsula.

In an isolated room of the White House three doctors under the direction of Surgeon-General Barnes made a last visual inspection of the gaunt body lying naked on a plank. At Barnes' direction, an incision was begun in the beard, on a level with the main connecting point of the upper portion of the ear. The knife was drawn smoothly upward along the hairline and then downward to the same point at the other ear. Thus freed, the upper scalp and forehead were peeled down over the lower face so there would be no visible evidence of the sawing that was about to commence.

The sound of the steel blade grinding its pathway around the skull was steady, sure, and methodical—a relentless sound, as of a million blue-clad troops carving their own bloody circles from the North to the South and back again, chewing like late-coming locusts on the carcass of a briefly living nation. And while Lincoln would lie among the honors of friends and the tears of family, there were others—refugees from burned-out homes and trampled crops—who mourned thousands not a fourth his age, with only crows and maggots to do their autopsies. Small comfort were his words of pity, to the slain; small hope were his promises of forgiveness, to the maimed.

The doctors laid aside the saw and removed the crown of the skull to expose the brain. Again the knife was brought into use, severing all bonds between the mind and the man, and then one of the doctors gently placed both of his hands deep down into the cranial cavity and firmly lifted away the tissue that had guided the lives of a nation through four long years of horror.

Abraham Lincoln was home in the White House from his last evening at the theatre.

ON MONDAY alterations were proceeding aboard the official presidential railroad car to transform it into an armored hearse as Lincoln was carried for the first of his many funerals into the East Room of the White House. Edward Spangler, a drunken roustabout at Ford's, was taken into custody that day while he ate his regular meal at a boardinghouse. Someone said he had called out, "Don't say which way he went," as Booth rode out the alleyway behind the theatre three nights before. Samuel Arnold and Michael O'Laughlin, both school friends of Booth's, were picked up later that morning; both of them had broken with the actor at the first mention of murder. In Maryland the drunken tavern keeper John Lloyd was arrested after directing pursuers along a route opposite to that taken by the assassin. That night Mrs. Mary Eugenia Surratt was arrested at her boardinghouse in Washington, and as she was being led away, Lewis Powell appeared out of desperation and coincidence upon her front porch. When his disguise proved faulty, he was also arrested.

On Tuesday, as the body of Abraham Lincoln was first placed upon public view, John Harrison Surratt, Jr., successfully escaped into Canada. The next day, at three-thirty in the afternoon, the grim cortege bearing Lincoln's body left the White House. A carpenter had been commissioned to build a catafalque. The embalmed body of the nation's first slain President was placed upon it in the rotunda of the Capitol Building, where he became the first American to lie in state under the newly completed dome. On either side of the casket were placed two muskets with bayonets, two carbines, and two crossed-sword bayonets.

The statue of Dying Tecumseh was draped, a railing covered

with black cloth obliterating it from view. All paintings were draped, and all the statues were covered except that of George Washington, which wore a black sash. The Great Dome of the Capitol, begun under the direction of onetime Secretary of War and U.S. senator Jefferson Davis, was draped to the floor.

A platform had been built around both sides of the casket, and 40,000 mourners passed to the face, looked down, and moved on. One by one, many of them placed flowers over the bearded face and body until the coffin was submerged in them.

On Thursday, as the funeral train was receiving the body of young Willie Lincoln, the President's son who had died of malaria two years earlier, George Atzerodt, a German carriage painter and sometime ferryboatman for Southern spies, was taken into custody at the farm of his cousin near Barnsville, Maryland. In Dr. Mudd's home was found the boot cut from the swollen leg of John Wilkes Booth, and that added another conspirator to the list of the captured.

That same Thursday night, Wilkes and his companion David Herold tried for the first time to cross the Potomac in a small rowboat and were turned back by the presence of a Union gunboat.

At six o'clock in the morning, April 21, dignitaries began assembling in the Rotunda, and soon the sergeants who had carried him from the White House again lifted the casket to carry him to the waiting railroad train. Soon the small funeral train pulled out of Washington, pausing to receive the respects of the citizens of Baltimore and then Harrisburg, and that night Booth's small boat carried him across Nanjemoy Creek to another encampment in Maryland.

On April 22 the little train passed Lancaster, Pennsylvania, where it was saluted by former President James Buchanan and the powerful Congressman Thaddeus Stevens. That night, Booth's little boat made it across the Potomac into Confederate Virginia.

There was a riot in crowd-jammed Philadelphia on April 23

as thousands pushed forward to view Lincoln's body, and in Washington Edwin Stanton issued an order "that the prisoners on board ironclads . . . for better security against conversation, shall have a canvas bag put over the head of each and tied around the neck, with a hole for proper breathing and eating, but not seeing. . . ."

On Monday, April 24, the little train pushed forward, picking up speed across New Jersey and infuriating the good fathers of Trenton by making theirs the only state capital not honored with a stop for a mourning procession, and, as the engine pulled into Newark, far to the south in Virginia John Wilkes Booth arrived at the small farm of William Garrett, seeking food and shelter.

Almost all eyes the next day were on New York City, where an elaborate bier had been built for a lengthy memorial procession down Manhattan Island. In Virginia, Union Captain Conger had "arrested" a Confederate soldier named Jett who confessed to leading Wilkes to Garrett's farm.

The troops were surrounding the little farm as the train moved out of New York City, heading for Albany, and in the first hours of April 26, Wilkes Booth died on the porch of the Garrett home.

The funeral train moved on from Albany to Buffalo, relentlessly passing the hundreds of small crowds at hundreds of rural crossings. On April 27, former President Millard Fillmore and young Congressman Grover Cleveland paid their respects to the slain man, while on a military ship in the Potomac a dentist and a doctor were busily poking into old scars and prying open the dead jaws of John Wilkes Booth.

On Friday, April 28, the body of Abraham Lincoln was being viewed in Cleveland, while in Washington the body of John Wilkes Booth was moved under cover of darkness into the deep bowels of the Old Penitentiary where, sewn into a blanket, he was lowered into a hidden grave.

The next day Lincoln was moved on into Columbus, Ohio,

the steam engine now pushing to maintain its schedule, and the conspirators were led in chains from the gunboats upon which they'd been held to separated cells in the Old Penitentiary. There they waited, shackled and hooded, while the funeral train sped westward through Indianapolis and Michigan City, through Chicago, and finally reached its last stop in Springfield on May 2. There Lincoln's horse, Old Bob, was waiting, along with his little dog, Fido, who had been left with friends when the President had gone away nearly five years before. Major General David Hunter, who had guarded the body on the long ride from Washington just as he had been assigned to guard the man on his journey toward immortality a half-decade earlier, now returned, alone, to the Capital. He had been appointed by Stanton to serve as presiding officer of the military commission established to try the accused conspirators.

BY THE TIME the military commission was convened, the government had reduced its suspects list to nine persons, only one of whom—John H. Surratt, Jr.—had appeared to be successful in escaping to Canada. The eight in custody, including Surratt's mother, were shackled and hooded in such a manner as to thoroughly prevent any but the most simple communication. The hoods were padded over the eyes and ears, and the prisoners' hands were bound in "stiff shackles," a form of handcuffs connected with a solid fourteen-inch bar of metal which makes writing difficult for a sighted person and virtually impossible for anyone blindfolded as they were. Moreover, they were housed in cells bordered on either side by empty cells, and were guarded by men under strict orders to have no conversation with them.

There had originally been ten conspirators apprehended but the government easily divided them into two groups. The first —eight of them—would defend their lives against testimony given by the other two—Louis Weichmann and John Lloyd. Both of these latter were tenants of Mrs. Surratt's—Weichmann a border in the home she maintained in Washington, and Lloyd the keeper of a tavern on the property she owned in Maryland.

Perhaps no band was ever quite so motley as the eight accused. They ranged from a propertied matriarch and a doctor to two alcoholic manual laborers. Of the lot of them, to this day only Powell and Herold are clearly and unquestionably members of the assassination party. Only Lincoln and Secretary Seward were attacked. Booth was alone at Ford's, while Powell was accompanied only by Herold at Seward's home. None of those three active participants saw any of the other accused between the criminal acts and the moment of capture, with the exception of Mudd. In short, none of the three active assassins were helped by any of the accused either to gain access to the victims or to escape afterwards. In a conspiracy, it is to be assumed that each conspirator has a role to play. Such an assumption by necessity lets even Dr. Mudd off the hook, since it is unlikely Booth would have planned on the need to have a broken leg fixed.

THUS CAME the prisoners to the dock. Facing them in the newly whitewashed courtroom set up in the Old Penitentiary were the nine military officers who would judge the prisoners in what one of the defense attorneys called "a contest in which a few lawyers were on one side, and the whole United States on the other—a case in which, of course, the verdict was known beforehand."

David Hunter, the presiding officer of the military commission, was a trusted confidant of Secretary of War Stanton as well as a close and warm friend of the slain President. His special charge, in orders signed by President Johnson, was to "establish such order or rules of proceeding as may avoid unnecessary delay, and conduce to the ends of public justice." Lest anyone doubt that the accused were to be given a speedy trial before execution, the President specifically decreed that "the said Commission . . . sit without regard to hours."

The remaining eight officers detailed to the military commission ranged in rank from lieutenant colonel to major general and in renown from Lew Wallace, who would become the author of *Ben Hur,* to Brigadier General T. M. Harris, a student of phrenology who apparently found Mudd guilty simply because "He had the bump of secretiveness largely developed."

Named specifically as judge advocate for the proceeding was the judge advocate general of the Army, Joseph Holt, a close friend of Stanton's and an arch radical* who was said to have been the author of the line that the trouble with the war was that "not enough women have been hanged."

"The commission has collectively an imposing appearance," wrote a reporter for the New York *World*:

> The face of Judge Holt is swarthy; he questions with slow utterance, holding the witness in his cold, measuring eye. Hunter, who sits at the opposite end of the table, shuts his eyes now and then, either to sleep or think, or both, and the other generals . . . watch for occasions to distinguish themselves.
>
> Excepting Judge Holt, the court has shown as little ability as could be expected from soldiers, placed in unenviable publicity, and upon a duty for which they are disqualified, both by education and acumen. Witness the lack of dignity in Hunter, who opened the court by a coarse allusion to "humbug chivalry"; of Lew Wallace, whose heat and intolerance were appropriately urged in the most exceptional English; of Howe, whose tirade against the rebel General Johnson was feeble as it was ungenerous. This court was needed to show us at least the petty tyranny of martial law and the pettiness of martial jurists. The counsel for the defense have just enough show to make the unfairness of the trial partake of hypocrisy. . . .

---

* "Radical" was a term used to describe those men—usually Republicans—who planned to impose harsh conditions for readmittance to the Union on the formerly Confederate states.

Whether the trial of the conspirators was any more unfair, viewed in hindsight, than others have been under similar circumstances is a moot question now, and it is similary irrelevant to ask whether any more witnesses perjured themselves against the Lincoln Eight than have done so against other alleged conspirators in other times, or whether any more use was made upon other occasions of irrelevant testimony about unsubstantiated and uncorroborated information. Certainly there are judges on record with less excuse for their predisposition to convict than the nine military men grown hardened by four years of killing and burdened by an acute sense that in the chaos of a leaderless nation the most needed thing was a demonstration of authority.

What is relevant is that in the course of presenting what is one of the most sloppy prosecution cases in American history, Holt gained convictions against all the accused without once shedding so much as a candle's - worth of light upon the motivation behind Booth's act or upon the role of John Surratt, who, it will be remembered, was being sought by the police less than five hours after the murder—making him at that time the only suspect besides Booth himself.

In Holt's professional, if not moral, defense, it is clear that he was saddled with a formal charge and specification of such Tower of Babel pretensions that it was always in danger of collapsing under its own weight. "For maliciously, unlawfully, and traitorously, and in aid of the existing armed rebellion against the United States of America," it charged the seven men and one woman with

> on or before the 6th day of March, A.D. 1865, and on divers other days between that day and the 15th day of April, A.D. 1865, combining, confederating, and conspiring together with one John H. Surratt, John Wilkes Booth, Jefferson Davis, George N. Sanders, Beverly Tucker, Jacob Thompson, William C. Cleary, Clement C. Clay, George Harper, George Young, and others unknown, to kill and murder,

The Missing Link / 159

within the Military Department of Washington, and within the fortified and intrenched lines thereof, Abraham Lincoln, late, and at the time of said combining, confederating, and conspiring, President of the United States of America, and Commander-in-Chief of the Army and Navy thereof; Andrew Johnson, now Vice President of the United States aforesaid; William H. Seward, Secretary of State of the United States aforesaid; and Ulysses S. Grant, Lieutenant-General of the Army of the United States aforesaid, then in command of the Armies of the United States under the direction of the said Abraham Lincoln. . . .

Aside from the fact that it is interesting to note John Surratt's name at the head of the list, it is important to understand that all of the names following Jefferson Davis' are those of Confederate operatives stationed in Canada. What the indictment alleges is that the accused were in a conspiracy with Davis and the Confederates in Canada to murder four officials of the U.S. government.

The difficulty with the indictment is twofold. First, there is not so much as a single shred of evidence that either Vice President Johnson or General Grant was ever a target of anyone in the group of accused, including Surratt and Booth. Second, the link to the conspiracy theory was John Surratt—who had served as a courier between the Confederates in Canada and the Richmond government—and Surratt, having successfully escaped, was unavailable to give the testimony which was essential to proving the conspiracy.

As a technical point of law, in a civil court the indictment could not be proven without Surratt. This may seem like a petty point, but it has vast implications. First, of course, failing to prove the indictment would virtually guarantee that any appellate court would throw out the convictions—and the government was therefore required to complete its case and to execute its sentences before such appeal could be made.* Second, it

* Following the conviction of Mary Surratt, a writ of habeas corpus was in fact issued by the federal court to stay her execution pending a civil review

indicates that the government believed it could indeed produce Surratt and his testimony before the end of the trial—and one is led inescapably to the suspicion that this was the primary reason for indicting Mary Surratt.

Assume, therefore, that the government has indicted Mary Surratt only to use her as bait, and that it is convinced her son's testimony can link the assassins to both the Canadian Confederates and to the highest officials of the Confederacy itself. If he does not rise to the bait, will it not be necessary to continue the charade and bring it as rapidly as possible to its conclusion?

The procedural rules of a military commission are not bound by the rules of evidence or the respect for the rights of the defendants that exist in the civil courts—and for men such as Stanton, who were far more concerned with holding the government together than with the rights of eight people they believed to be traitors, it was unquestionably preferable to keep the case in a military forum where the introduction of evidence could be controlled and the foregone conclusion quickly reached. But there was a growing clamor—spearheaded by the chief defense attorney, Reverdy Johnson—for a trial before a civil judge and jury. As later appellate decisions proved,* the government had good reason to fear that those favoring a civil trial were legally correct—and that, therefore, the defendants needed to be promptly led to the gallows before the cases could be taken over by the civil courts.

Given only two weeks to prepare for the prosecution of a complex conspiracy case, Judge Advocate General Holt was forced to present a scattergun prosecution sufficient to allow

---

of the case. President Andrew Johnson suspended her constitutional right to such a writ (as, to be fair, Lincoln himself had done from time to time during the war). Supreme Court Chief Justice Taney, however, had ruled —in Circuit Session—as early as 1861 that such suspension of fundamental rights amounted to "usurpation" (17 Fed. Cas. 144).

* In 1867, the Supreme Court ruled, in *ex parte Milligan*, that military tribunals could not be convened where the civil courts were fully functioning. The civil courts were fully functioning in Washington during the trial of the assassination conspirators.

the commission to send half the accused to their deaths and the remainder to prison—which was, after all, what he was supposed to do. But in doing it he was required to utilize dubious evidence in some areas and to suppress valid evidence in other areas, and the upshot of it all was to create a muddled history filled with blind leads and large questions.

Holt could not, to use a perfect example, probe too deeply into the life of John Wilkes Booth without revealing a secret which was successfully kept quiet for a half century. The judge advocate did establish that Booth was near the President on Inauguration Day, but he could not develop the point without revealing that the actor had gained access to the VIP platform on a pass received from the father of his secret fiancée, Lucy Hale. Two months before the assassination, as Booth kept his brother Edwin awake late into the night helping him compose a Valentine's Day love poem to Lucy, her mother and father were dining handsomely in the White House, celebrating Senator Hale's forthcoming retirement as a ranking legislator in order to accept an appointment as the new U.S. ambassador to Spain. There is no record of how Lucy reacted when the newspapers carried the story that Ella Turner, Booth's mistress, had attempted suicide the day after the assassination, but she is rumored to have written Edwin Booth that she was prepared to marry his brother even upon the gallows. No one in Washington would have ruined her life, or that of her popular and respected father, by delving too deeply into Wilkes Booth's activities in Washington.

Holt's strongest arguments, therefore, relied upon the questionable testimony of men with their own axes to grind. John Lloyd and Louis Weichmann—whose joint testimony sent Mary Surratt to the hangman—were each threatened with indictment unless they testified, and the dubious quality of such testimony was underscored when Lloyd was proven to have been falling-down-drunk during the period covered by his testimony. There were other prosecution witnesses equally if not more guilty than the accused—chief among them Willie Jett, one of the Confederate soldiers who helped Booth escape—whose testimony no doubt followed a deal with the prosecution. Jett freely admitted helping to hide Booth even though he was aware that Booth was the assassin—and providing such assistance was a capital crime. But it was also Jett who most likely led the troops to Garrett's farm, and, as in many instances involving Secret Service Chief Lafayette Baker,* one senses chicanery.

Out of this confusion of evidence produced in haste and pending too often upon men's personal fears or ambitions came convictions which totally ignored the primary charge of the trial: That there was a conspiracy "with one John H. Surratt, John Wilkes Booth, Jefferson Davis," and several Confederate operatives in Canada "to kill and murder . . . Abraham Lincoln, late, and . . . William H. Seward, Secretary of State . . ."

THE ACCUSED sat before their judges from May 9, 1865, until June 30 of the same year, when their sentences were handed down, and each time they entered the specially built "courtroom" it was as if eight copies of Marley's Ghost had been created to shuffle by in a line with their chains rattling. Their hoods removed for each appearance, they were kept separated, each from the others, by an armed and blue-clad soldier. Some misplaced sense of chivalry had led to the chains being removed from Mrs. Surratt, at least in public. The next most quiet of the prisoners was the biggest of them all, Lewis Powell, who entered court each day in his stockings because his feet had swollen too much under the irritation of his shackles to fit any longer in his boots.

The son of a Florida Baptist minister, Lewis Thornton Pow-

---

* A liar and schemer, Baker tried his best to capture the $100,000 reward for Booth's head—including the forging of reward posters. He specifically sent Conger and Baker to Port Royal—and no one ever discovered his source of information that Booth was there.

ell had lost two brothers during the war, and was himself a veteran of both regular and irregular service in the Confederacy. Perfectly postured throughout the trial, he consistently wore a dark knit pull-on shirt exposing a side-show strong man's physique, and freely confessed his guilt along with a desire that they "hang me quick." A professed God-fearing man too young to show a discernible beard, he was remembered to have prayed daily while claiming that although he had sought to kill Secretary Seward he had nevertheless done no wrong, since killing of any kind is justified during wartime.

Powell had a disconcerting habit of steadfastly returning the curious stares of the onlookers, and when these curiosity seekers turned from his gaze in embarrassment they invariably sought the second most notorious of the conspirators—Mary Eugenia Surratt.*

Virtually hidden behind a black veil and the palm leaf fan she clutched in a black-mittened hand, Mary Surratt was known to be a handsome woman of forty-five and a decent kindly Christian woman of high repute—despite being a Catholic, a Confederate, and a murderess, none of which descriptions was ever taken other than for granted, and in some circles all of which were considered synonymous. She never spoke, seldom moved, and seemed for that matter to spend the entire trial staring intently at the floor.

Louis Weichmann testified that her son, along with Powell and Booth, came and went together from her house at odd hours. It was damning testimony, even though it was muted a bit by the obvious pressure Weichmann was under to be either an effective witness or one of the accused himself. He helped put her on the gallows, however, by testifying that he had ridden with her to the tavern in Maryland on the assassination afternoon while she delivered a spyglass to John Lloyd and told

---

* As Powell walked to the gallows, he continued to insist that Mrs. Surratt had not known of the assassination plot to which he'd freely confessed his own guilt.

him to "have the shooting irons ready" because they would be called for that very night.

Lloyd, for his part, put the noose about her neck by corroborating Weichmann's testimony, and even though the defense established that Lloyd had been too drunk to remember much, if anything, of that day, it didn't help mitigate the testimony.*

At the age of thirty-two, Dr. Samuel Mudd was already balding, which revealed the bump so important to one of the judges, and aided the impression of general sneakiness which the other judges took into account. The testimony against him—including two visits with Booth before the actor appeared at the doctor's home to have his broken leg fixed—was hardly needed by the court to find him guilty, though the defense was able to save his life.†

Davie Herold's guilt was never in doubt.

Poor George Atzerodt was alleged to have been too scared to

---

* Under our system of laws, however, a person is guilty beyond reasonable doubt—or else is not guilty. Mary Surratt was more than the first woman slain for conspiracy to assassinate a President; she was, in fact, slain without a shred of evidence pointing to her guilt. Certainly Weichmann rode with her to her Maryland tavern, and he probably saw her say something to Lloyd. Her son was a spy, and like any good mother, she would help her son (particularly since she approved his politics, as the trial did demonstrate). Weichmann's and Lloyd's evidence is no evidence at all—even if their observations were correct, there isn't a single clue that indicates she understood the reasons behind her actions.

Mary Surratt was innocent, by every definition of American justice. But she was only bait. The government was after bigger fish—and fisherman don't mind losing bait.

† Mudd's is a tragic and complex case. His meetings with Booth before the assassination strongly implicate him as an active member of the Confederate underground operating in the Maryland Peninsula, a likelihood strongly supported by the readiness with which Booth turned to him for treatment of the actor's broken leg. In this case, however, Mudd was not on trial as a Confederate but as an assassin. Following a day of indecision, the doctor had effectively turned himself in on the Sunday following the assassination when he asked a relative to notify federal troops of a disguised late-night caller with a broken leg. It may well have been that Mudd was reluctant to turn in a former comrade; more likely, however, he was torn between the equally lethal prospects of a Union hangman and the revenge of Confederate guerrillas. His indecision nearly cost him his life.

carry out his mission of murdering Vice President Johnson, and as the squat and neckless German immigrant waddled into court each day, "inscrutable as some Eastern idol," it was never doubted that such was the case.

Edward Spangler, who was accused of yelling, "Don't tell them which way he went!" as Booth rode away from the rear of the theatre that night, seemed to be suffering from delirium tremens through much of the trial. Along with Dr. Mudd, he would be spared the gallows, though not prison, and on his deathbed years later he would still be proclaiming his innocence.

Sam Arnold and Michael O'Laughlin—Booth's boyhood friends—looked like decent and likable young men, and the evidence against them was more thin than a gallows-rope, so they would join Mudd and Spangler in prison.*

On July 6, 1865, in nearly unbearable heat, the four condemned prisoners—Mary Surratt, Davie Herold, Lewis Powell, and George Atzerodt—were led up the steps of a gallows built to carry all of them at once out of this world. Two soldiers had been detailed to knock the supports from under the platform, and when they did so three of the prisoners died instantly.

Lewis Powell's knot was set wrong so that it failed to break his neck, and therefore the man who had asked only that they "hang me quick" dangled and writhed for a while as he strangled.

A few yards away, hidden in an unmarked grave, was the body of John Wilkes Booth. And left dangling higher than Lewis Powell was the charge for which all four had died—did they, indeed, conspire "with one John H. Surratt, John Wilkes Booth, Jefferson Davis," and Confederate operatives in Can-

---

* The four men would be sent to a place popularly called "America's Devil's Island"—a swampy hellhole in the Florida Keys known as the Dry Tortugas. There, after more than two years, a yellow fever epidemic took the lives of Michael O'Laughlin and most of the prison's medical staff. For his heroism working round the clock to treat inmates and prison staff, Dr. Samuel A. Mudd was granted a presidential pardon, as were his assistants, Samuel Arnold and Ned Spangler.

ada, "to kill and murder . . . Abraham Lincoln, late, and . . . William H. Seward, Secretary of State. . . ."

The case against George Atzerodt—even after a century—remains weak. All of the available evidence indicates only that Atzerodt was registered as occupying a room in Andrew Johnson's hotel on the night of the assassination. There is no evidence that he knew why, and there is considerable circumstantial evidence indicating that he was in fact set up as a patsy to mislead the police following the assassination.

Davie Herold was unquestionably with Booth at the time the assassin was killed—and with Lewis Powell outside Seward's home just before Powell attempted to kill the Secretary of State.

There is no question that John Wilkes Booth shot and killed Abraham Lincoln.

In the shadows of the conspiracy to kill Lincoln and Seward is John Harrison Surratt, Jr. The eternal spy, John Surratt went to his grave from natural causes after many years maintaining silence about the assassination. But as with Rome, all roads concerning the assassination lead to John Surratt. This key spy and courier for the Confederacy between Richmond and Montreal left Canada three days before the assassination and returned to it three days later. A dozen witnesses placed him in Washington on the day of the killing.

Finally, in the mystery of the assassination hangs the question of why there was a major attempt to murder Secretary of State Seward—and no other member of the government except Lincoln. In the minds of most Southern patriots, Seward was by no means the chief enemy; other candidates would have filled the bill much more suitably—such as General Grant, Vice President Andrew Johnson, or Secretary of War Edwin Stanton. These three men—Grant the butcher, Johnson the pro-Union former Southern senator, and the flagrantly radical Stanton—would have been far more appropriate secondary targets were John Wilkes Booth maddened by a desire for vengeance against the enemies of the South. There is not a shred of evidence to indicate that an attack was contemplated against any of them.

Instead, the brawny Lewis Powell was sent with a heavy pistol and a bowie knife to murder a crippled old man as he slept in his sickbed: William H. Seward, the only major official of the Union government whose activities had not been directed toward the military suppression of the South. To the contrary, William Seward's only direct involvement with the Confederacy had been a skillful thwarting of repeated attempts by Confederate operatives in Montreal to create hostilities between the United States, Canada and England. Because the government was moving hastily at the trial of the conspirators, because it was functioning under enormous political pressure, because it was being conducted by impassioned men, a kangaroo-style military tribunal did in fact mete out sentences without regard for justice—and it undoubtedly sent Mary Surratt unfairly to the gallows. The government, as well, failed by any detached legal standard to prove its indictments.

Textbooks for over a century have therefore propagated the legend that John Wilkes Booth was a madman who acted in an impulsive and perhaps drunken hour to destroy our greatest President. The irony is that the indictment itself is far closer to the truth, at least in the cases of Herold and Powell, because they did indeed conspire "with one John H. Surratt, John Wilkes Booth," and Confederate operatives in Canada "to kill and murder . . . Abraham Lincoln, late, and . . . William H. Seward, Secretary of State . . ."

For so extraordinary a scheme, the government had been able to indict only eight nonentities and send but four of these to the gallows.

The truth is that the government was after bigger fish, and, indeed, Jefferson Davis himself spent the duration of the trial shackled in solitary confinement in a Southern prison. The government built a circumstantial case against him, noting that Booth's cipher was the same as that used by Confederate Secretary of State Benjamin, accepting testimony that Surratt in his last visit to Richmond had spoken with both Benjamin and Davis, even placing in the record allegations that Davis had reacted with pleasure upon hearing the news of Lincoln's death. In time, as national passions were calmed, fewer and fewer citizens would come to believe in Davis' alleged complicity—and he would live out his days an honored, if embittered, man. But at the time, linking him to the assassination was clearly the intent of Stanton and Holt.

The government gambled that the linking element—embodied in the form of the twenty-three-year-old secret courier who had left Davis and Benjamin in early April for Montreal, then left Montreal to communicate with Booth during the three days before the murder—would present himself before the trial's end, if only to save the life of his mother. Perhaps if Stanton and Holt had known him better they would have realized it was a pointless gamble—a man doesn't survive for three years as a spy behind the enemy's lines by nurturing his softnesses.

It is doubtful that even Surratt—had he given honest testimony—could have put Davis upon the scaffold. But without such testimony, the government could do little but hold the Confederate president in prison for a few months while debating the wisdom of putting him on trial for treason. As time passed—and as passions and politics changed—the people grew to believe not only in Davis' innocence, but in the innocence, as well, of Mary Surratt. As two years passed, it became more openly charged that Stanton had railroaded her to the gallows.

And at the end of those two years, John Surratt would have his day in court.

CHAPTER XIV

Postmortem

NEARLY ONE AND A HALF YEARS after the death of John Wilkes Booth and the execution of those convicted as his co-conspirators, the U.S. steamship *Swatara* anchored off Alexandria, Egypt, to board an infamous cargo.

"I saw him when he was brought aboard as a prisoner," George D. F. Barton, U.S. Navy paymaster, remembered. "I heard he was coming, and went on deck to see him when he came aboard."

Disguised in the uniform of a papal guard, John H. Surratt, Jr., had been at last captured in Egypt. "After we took him aboard," paymaster Barton described it later, at Surratt's trial, "we went to Port Mahon, expecting to find the Admiral there . . . and then from there to Villa Franca, where we found the Admiral, and we were then ordered to this country and came direct, stopping at Madeira for coal. We arrived in sight of

Cape Henry on the 18th of February, and then came up the river, and delivered him here in Washington."

He still wore the disguise he had worn when escaping from Italy to Egypt: "it is the regular Zouave dress," Barton recalled, "very much the same as we have here—blue pants, red trimmings, blue Zouave jacket, fez cap, white gaiters, and a sash."

Nearly two years earlier, when he had run away, the reward posters named him second only to Booth in desirability—and put a price of $25,000 on his head. But there was no reward when he was finally taken into custody; for that matter, the government seemed more reluctant than Surratt himself to have him in chains.

HAVING BEEN HIDDEN AWAY in a monastery outside Montreal throughout the trial of his mother two years earlier, Surratt had finally budged from his secluded safety in September 1865, when he sailed for Liverpool. His presence in England was soon discovered and reported to the U.S. consul. In response to the consul's requests for instructions in the matter, State Department officials consulted with Stanton and Holt before replying that it was believed "advisable that no action be taken."

Only a few weeks earlier, all the Federal government's energies and powers had been concentrated solely upon bringing John Surratt's mother and the other "co-conspirators" to the hangman. Only a few weeks before that, the largest manhunt in the nation's history had tracked John Booth to his death—and only a short time ago agents sent into Canada had barely missed capturing their prey: John Surratt himself.

Now that same government believed it "advisable that no action be taken."

As in the case of the original conspiracy trial, the series of curious positions taken by the government regarding John Surratt can only be understood in the light of a dismal combination of statesmanship and common self-protective politics.

It must be remembered that Secretary of State William Seward had lain at death's door throughout most of the summer, recovering from both the carriage accident and Powell's furious attack. As rapidly as he became able to resume his duties he had turned his energies to foreign affairs—and particularly to returning relationships with England toward some setting of normalcy.

Busily pressing U.S. claims for reimbursement for financial losses caused by English assistance to the Confederacy, and only freshly relieved from the fear of war with Victoria's government, Seward could hardly afford an extradition fight so long as Surratt was on English soil. After spending the last four years of his life working hard to keep American Anglophobia from sparking a war, he had little interest in a renewal of it if faced with a British refusal to turn Surratt over on demand.

This explanation is given credence by subsequent events. On October 25, 1865, the State Department received a cable which began: "It is Surratt's intention to go to Rome . . . If an officer could proceed to England . . . I have no doubt but that Surratt's arrest might be effected. . . ."

Thus partially freed to move, Seward on November 13 wrote to the Attorney General, requesting him to "procure an indictment against the said John H. Surratt as soon as convenient, with the view to demand his surrender." But, so long as Surratt remained in England, the Secretary of State had no intention of pressing the matter.*

In what was perhaps a move undertaken at Seward's request in order to diminish the zeal of the informer who was pressing for Surratt's immediate arrest, Edwin Stanton on November 24 issued an order noting that "the reward offered for the arrest of . . . . John H. Surratt is revoked."

---

* A congressional committee would later report: "Whether an indictment was procured does not appear from the testimony, but it does appear that no demand for the surrender of Surratt was ever made upon the English Government."

Seward had to wait five more months before becoming completely free to deal with Surratt. On April 23, 1866, the American minister to Rome transmitted to Washington the information that John Surratt had enlisted in the service of the Pope under the name of John Watson. The news took a month to reach Washington, and promptly on May 28 Seward recommended to Stanton that a special agent be sent to Rome to demand the fugitive's surrender.

But while events were making it possible for Seward to move against Surratt, other events were making Edwin Stanton increasingly reluctant to see the young spy brought to justice. In April 1866, the Supreme Court handed down a preliminary judgment in *ex parte Milligan* requiring the army to free its prisoner, Lambdin P. Milligan, and promising to issue a broad, constitutionally based opinion in the matter beginning with its next regular session in December. For Stanton, it was a double blow.

The question at issue in *Milligan* was whether or not a military commission could put civilians on trial in a district in which the civil courts were sitting—and the preliminary judgment strongly obligated Stanton to allow Surratt to stand trial before a jury of his peers, rather than one of soldiers. The judgment was a warning that in December the Court would hold that a military commission could not sit in such civilian cases, and its implications were that the Lincoln conspirators had been sent to the gallows illegally.

It was a tragically moot point in their instance, but to Stanton it was a virtual guarantee that John Surratt could not be dispatched with quite the same ease as his mother.

The ghost of Mary Surratt was beginning to cast an ever-widening shadow in political Washington. The public's shock over her death—of the hanging of the first woman ever to be executed—had dealt Stanton a political black eye that was severely damaging to him in the growing wars between President Andrew Johnson and Stanton's fellow Radical Republicans.

Postmortem / 173

WHEN THE NINE MILITARY MEN who had sat as judges in the conspiracy trial had gathered in privacy to decide the fates of the accused, two votes had been taken for each prisoner. A simple majority was sufficient for conviction, but two-thirds was required to impose a death sentence. The military men had balked at sending the woman to her doom, and Judge Advocate General Holt had argued, futilely, trying to win over the required six of them for the hangman. Then he had asked that they recess overnight without rendering a decision.

Holt returned the next day—after conferring with Stanton—offering a new line of argument and a suggestion. To not sentence her to die, he said, would be to invite future assassins to seek out women as their triggermen. But, he pointed out, the commission's sentence had to be affirmed by the President, and therefore those officers who wished the sentence to be commuted could try to influence the President by a private petition for mercy. The military commission bought the suggestion, voted as Holt wanted and then drew up and signed the mercy request.

Days later, on July 6, 1865, a reporter walked into the courtyard of the Old Penitentiary and drew back in surprise when he counted four nooses hanging from the gallows. "You mean there are four of them?" he asked, incredulous. It was unbelievable to everyone that Mrs. Surratt would still die. Inside his cell Lewis Powell was telling his guards exactly the same story that Mary Surratt was confessing to her priest that noontime—she was unaware of the death plot.

Relays of horsemen were kept waiting between the gallows and the White House all that morning, and even after the hour appointed for the execution itself, since the commander-in-charge was certain the commutation was coming, and that it was only delayed. At last, unable to wait any longer, he gave the command that caused her death, and the horsemen in the relay were sent back to their barracks.

The President had sent no commutation flying from one of their hands to the next—and until his dying day Andrew Johnson swore that he had never seen, nor had he ever been told about, the petition.

Few others saw it either. It wasn't until the 1920's that it was accidentally found lying on a shelf under a staircase in the old War Department building. The petition was written on the flip side of the last page of Judge Advocate General Holt's summary report to the President on the trial. Johnson had read through each page of the report and had signed it below the commission's recommendations for sentencing, about halfway down the last page. If he had turned that last page over and then turned the document upside down, he would have been able to read the mercy petition. Perhaps he did so and ignored it, but perhaps a man who has read through a score of pages with writing on only one side is unlikely to check out the back of the last page. Curious men might also note that the officers who signed the mercy petition did so upon a clean sheet of paper—and then might wonder why Holt turned it over to write the last page of his report on its flip side.

Whether Stanton and Holt conspired to keep Johnson from having the opportunity to exercise clemency will no doubt remain a speculation—but by the same token, it was being openly debated as the summer of 1866 passed into fall. And Stanton had even greater worries.

Wilkes Booth's diary—with its numerous reflections about his motives and its allusions that he had acted alone—would have been a bombshell exploding in the middle of the prosecution's case if the defense had heard about it during Mary Surratt's trial. It had been suppressed ever since being turned over to Stanton. Its discovery now could lead to very embarrassing questions.

FINALLY, IN THE FALL OF 1866, events were taken out of Stanton's hands. The Vatican itself attempted to apprehend its mysterious employee, "John Watson." Surratt escaped only by jumping a wall. But after the incident, too many others—in foreign governments, in the State Department, and in Congress —knew that Surratt could be captured to make further delays possible. He *had* to be taken into custody, and this was promptly done in November, almost as soon as Surratt set foot in Alexandria. On February 21, three days after the *Swatara* reached Washington, he was turned over to the authorities for trial.

Two weeks earlier, on February 7, 1867, onetime Secret Service Chief Lafayette Baker, no loyal friend of Stanton's or of anyone else, and a not-overly-reliable witness under any circumstances, had taken the stand before a congressional hearing to declare that Wilkes Booth had kept a diary during the escape, and that Baker had given it intact to Stanton. But when the War Secretary—upon the committee's insistence— produced the diary, eighteen pages were missing, and many were led to charge openly that these pages confirmed the innocence of Mrs. Surratt and had therefore been destroyed.*

Stanton was under intense political pressure. The Black Republicans were squaring off against Democratic President Andrew Johnson in a power brawl that would establish political control of the United States for the next quarter-century. One of the most powerful Black Republican leaders—Edwin Stanton—sat within the President's Cabinet, and in March, immediately after Surratt had been returned and the diary made public, the Congress had passed the Tenure of Office Act to prevent Johnson from firing him without first gaining congressional consent.†

---

* Wilkes is likely to have used some of the diary pages as note paper, and may well have used all the missing pages himself for such purposes. But an inspection of the binding remnants indicates most were removed in bulk, since the rip marks are precisely the same for two separate groups of pages. Pencil marks in the bindings do indicate that there was writing on the removed pages.
† On February 21, 1868, Johnson would fire Stanton anyway—and three days later the House voted eleven Articles of Impeachment, nine of which

Against such a backdrop, any evidence helping a suspicious public confirm Stanton's heavy-handed and perhaps illegal persecution of Mrs. Surratt would have had vast implications not only for the War Secretary but for the entire Republican Party itself. It is beyond belief to assume that under such conditions John Surratt's trial would be unmarked by the stain of party politics.

John Surratt's trial would unquestionably be a retrial of his mother. And if she was thus retrospectively to be found innocent, her death would be laid no longer on the balancing scale of the Republic's injuries, but rather at the vengeful door of the War Secretary, who Lincoln called "my Mars."

It is little wonder that Stanton looked forward to the trial without relish. The government, therefore, exhibited no greater haste in bringing Surratt to trial than it had exhibited in gaining custody of him, and it was not until June 10, 1867, that the trial began, under an indictment charging

> that the said John Wilkes Booth, late of the county aforesaid, and the said John H. Surratt, late of the county aforesaid, and the said David E. Herold, late of the county aforesaid, and the said George A. Atzerodt, late of the county aforesaid, and the said Lewis Payne, late of the county aforesaid and the said Mary E. Surratt, late of the county aforesaid, together with divers other persons to the jurors aforesaid unknown, on the said fourteenth day of April, in the year of our Lord one thousand eight hundred and sixty-five, at the county of Washington aforesaid, unlawfully and wickedly did combine, confederate, and conspire and agree together feloniously to kill and murder one Abraham Lincoln....

But the government had not run out of delaying tactics. Its first action was to challenge the legality of the selection of veniremen from whom the jury would be chosen. Following a

---

stemmed from Stanton's dismissal. Acting on those Articles, the Senate majority failed by only one vote to get the two-thirds required for Andrew Johnson's removal from office.

line of argument that the strictest interpretation of an 1862 law prescribing the manner of impaneling a jury in Washington had not been followed—even though the same procedure used throughout the period from 1862 to 1867 had been followed in Surratt's case—the federal prosecutors were able to have the regular jury dismissed.

Federal marshals were now sent into the streets to recruit talesmen—which is to say, to grab whomever they wished for impressment into jury service. The fear of having such practices result in the packing of a jury by the marshal's impressing only men who would convict was among the reasons for passing the 1862 law, which the prosecutors claimed had not been used properly—and, in fact, the fear of the defense attorneys was that precisely such a purpose had been in the minds of the prosecutors all along.

It may have been so—but there was a more important motive. Under another Washington law, any jury which was not fully impaneled by the end of a sitting court's term would be dismissed and a new trial date would have to be set, following a first-come-first-served docketing rule. In effect, a case docketed late in a term would have to quickly impanel its jury or else go to the bottom of the list for a trial date during the following term—a delay of several months at best. Surratt's case had begun on June 10; the new court session was scheduled to begin on June 17.

Surratt's defense lawyers—determined to insure Surratt a trial rather than see him sit in jail for yet more months without one—succeeded in overcoming this policy of prosecutorial delays, and just before midnight of the final day of the old court's term, Saturday, June 15, the final juror was sworn.

FOR FIFTY-THREE STIFLING DAYS of Washington's swampy summer—from June 10 to August 7—the jury listened to the evidence. It traced John Surratt from the city of Washington on the day President Lincoln was shot, to his hideout in Canada, and from there to Europe. Along the way, the evidence suggested, the careful spy had sometimes talked too much.

Eyewitnesses swore he had spoken of his travels with the mysterious Mrs. Slater—and of the time when the party, in Virginia, came across a band of half-starved escaped Union prisoners. "Let us shoot the damn Yankee soldiers," Mrs. Slater had commanded, and the members of the group, including Surratt, had drawn their revolvers to obey.

Surratt claimed to have received money in Richmond from Secretary of State Benjamin upon several occasions. A witness remembered two amounts—$30,000 and $70,000, received "while he was in Richmond just a few days previous to its fall—I should say the week immediately previous to the fall of Richmond." Jacob Thompson deposited over $100,000 in a Montreal bank on April 6, 1865—the same day John Surratt arrived in Montreal from Richmond.

The same witness remembered Surratt saying in England that "he would shoot the first officer that layed (sic) his hand on him" because, in Surratt's words, "I would rather be hanged by an English hangman than by a Yankee one, because I know very well if ever I go back to the United States I shall swing."

Another witness recalled Surratt telling him that "he had done more things than I was aware of, and that very likely if I knew, it would make my eyes stare, or something to that effect." Once, in the South, Surratt "was with a regiment of Rebel soldiers one evening; then after sunset he and some others went into an orchard or garden close by and took some fruit; that while sitting and eating those fruits they heard the ticking of a telegraphic machine, or at least what they supposed to be a telegraphic machine; that they came down to the headquarters of the regiment and reported it; that the party in command ordered some of the soldiers to go to the house which was connected with the orchard and search; that in the garret of the house, in a closet, they found a Union soldier; that they found out he was working an underground telegraph; and that they took him down and shot him, or hanged him, I forget which...."

In another instance, Surratt allegedly spoke of an evening when he and other spys were "crossing the Potomac in a boat; it was in the evening, I believe; that they were perceived by a gunboat and hailed; they were ordered to surrender, or else they would be fired upon. They immediately said they would surrender. The gunboat sent a small boat to them. They waited until the small boat came immediately alongside, and then fired into them, and afterwards escaped themselves to the shore...."

What the testimony suggests, of course, is that John Surratt was not a very nice young man. Throughout the war he had lived with his family—first at the farm and tavern near Bryantown in the Maryland Peninsula toward which John Booth headed on the first leg of his escape, and then, after his father's death, in the boardinghouse on H Street, near Ford's Theatre, where the plotters had gathered. During the war, as well, he had steadily risen in the Confederate underground from the status of an occasional messenger to that of a respected courier. As he later told it, he "was mostly engaged in sending information regarding the movements of the United States Army stationed in Washington and elsewhere, and carrying despatches to the Confederate boats on the Potomac." It was an expectedly modest description.

The prosecution had little difficulty proving that John Surratt was a courier and spy for the Confederacy, but it must be remembered that he was indicted for murder rather than for a lack of patriotism. The prosecution tried to close its case by turning to the indictment itself.

During the period in which the assassination took place, John Sangston had been the desk clerk at a Montreal hotel called St. Lawrence Hall. He testified that on the afternoon of April 12, 1865, John Surratt "left the house for the New York train . . . at three o'clock and returned on April 18" but "did not stay any time at all. I do not know how long he did stay. He just came into the house and did not stay any time. . . . He went in the city somewhere, I believe."

Another witness testified to being told by Surratt that "I was disguised so that nobody would take me for an American; I looked like an Englishman; I had a scarf over my shoulders."

After the trial, Surratt himself described the disguise he wore when he slipped back cross the Canadian border on April 18: "I had provided myself with an oxford-cut jacket and round-top hat peculiar to Canada at that time. . . . One of the detectives approached me, stared me directly in the face, and I looked him quietly back. In a few moments I was speeding on my way to Montreal. . . ."

Surratt's corroboration of the witness's description lends credence to the witness's earlier exchange with the prosecution attorney: "I asked the prisoner how he got out from Washington," the witness testified at the trial, "if he had a hard time since he had left? He told me he had very hard times, and at other times. . . ."

"How did he say he got out from Washington?" the prosecutor asked.

"He told me he left that night."

"What night?"

"The night of the assassination," the witness replied, "or the next morning; I am not positive which."

All together, twelve witnesses placed John Surratt in Washington on the day of the assassination. The defense could find only one eyewitness to back Surratt's contention that he had gotten no closer to Washington than Elmira, New York, had telegraphed Booth, and when he received no answer, had returned to Montreal.

Surratt's vigorous and hard-working defense attorneys refused to put their client on the stand and, to their credit, were able to cast doubt upon the veracity of some—but not all—of the prosecution's evidence. Casting doubt upon some of it, however, was sufficient.

The defense was able to demonstrate that enough of the prosecution's witnesses had perjured themselves to cast doubt upon the testimony of them all. Undoubtedly aided by the two years of growing public doubt regarding Mrs. Surratt's guilt—and by the blatancy of the judge's pro-prosecution bias at John Surratt's trial—the defense cracked the government's case just enough that on Saturday, August 10, 1867, the jury sent a note to the judge:

> The jury in the case of the United States vs. John H. Surratt most respectfully state that they stand precisely now as when they first ballotted upon entering the room, nearly equally divided, and they are firmly convinced that they cannot possibly make a verdict. We deem it our duty to the court, to the country, and in view of the condition of our private affairs, and situation of our families, and in view of the fact that the health of several of our number is becoming seriously impaired under the protracted confinement, to make this statement, to ask your honor to dismiss us at once.

The defense protested dismissing the jury, believing no doubt that acquittal was possible and that even a guilty verdict would be reversed in the appellate courts.* The prosecution, however, readily assented when the judge adjourned the court and sent the jurymen back to their private businesses. The government had every reason to be pleased with a hung jury—pressured by public opinion to bring John Surratt to trial, it had done so; and

---

* A very large part of Surratt's trial was occupied with arguments involving the defense, the prosecution, and the bench itself regarding points of law. At several dozen points—beginning with the selection of the jury, continuing through questions of admissible evidence and concluding with the final grounds of dismissal of the jury—the defense noted its objections for inclusion in the official record. Clearly, Surratt's attorneys were laying the basis for an appeal based on judicial error, and given the obvious bias of the judge, they were likely to win such an appeal.

Surratt had not taken the stand in his own defense, had not made himself liable to cross-examination.

And, with a hung jury, John Surratt could be brought to trial again at any time the government wished to do so—such as in the event he ever opened his mouth and began telling his full story.

John Surratt carried his secrets—if he had any—to the grave. But half the jury believed him to be a conspirator, presumably "beyond a shadow of a doubt," and history must at least take note that on April 12, exactly three days before the assassination, he had left Canada and exactly three days after the assassination had taken place, he had returned to Canada in disguise.

THE TRUTH regarding our first assassination is a difficult case to present. First of all, the politics of Reconstruction blurred much of it, and, sadly, because too many dishonest men played major roles in that Reconstruction period.

Into this latter category were men like Lafayette Baker, head of the U.S. Secret Service—who saw $100,000 in reward money and went after it. Because of his avarice, we shall never really know how Booth was tracked to Garrett's little farm, nor shall we ever know why Willie Jett and his two fellow "Confederate soldiers" were not prosecuted for helping to hide Booth. Because of the politics of Reconstruction, we shall also never know how complete Wilkes' diary was, we shall never know whether Booth or Stanton ripped the pages from the assassin's diary, and we shall never know "beyond a shadow of a doubt" whether or not John Surratt was the author of the plot or merely a messenger somehow involved in it. But the important point is that all of the trails always end up at the same point—Montreal. Trace John Surratt's known career right up to April 18, 1865, and the conspiracy to murder Lincoln points to Montreal. Trace the known facts about Lewis Powell, and they point to Montreal. Trace the known potential reasons for

Postmortem / 183

killing Seward and they point to Montreal. Trace Booth's involvement in the conspiracy and it points to Montreal.

Probe more deeply. The government's coverups in the first trial—the only possible motive for the prosecution of Mrs. Surratt is to lure her son back to testify. About what? About Montreal—and about Confederate involvement in the killing. Look into reasons for Seward dragging his feet about getting Surratt extradited—a man who tried to have him murdered!—and you bump into fears that what Surratt knows may create international problems. Again, Montreal.

Finally, look at the original indictment itself. It charges a conspiracy involving those convicted along with Booth and Surratt and Jefferson Davis himself to have plotted with seven Confederate agents operating from Montreal.

All of the evidence suggests that John Harrison Surratt, Jr., either alone or with others, came up with an idea some time between April 9 and April 12. The idea was to have Booth use his name to get close enough to Lincoln for the killing, and to have Powell kill Seward at the same time. On April 12, Surratt left Canada with that plot in mind, and with the mission of leading Booth safely back to Canada.

If the message had come to Booth from anywhere but Canada it would probably not have included Seward. The plot must have included an escape plan—with Atzerodt in Washington, Booth must have been planning to go north, and nobody but Surratt could help in such an escape.

It is equally likely that no court sitting in civil session could convict Surratt—with politicians hiding evidence, his primary co-conspirators Booth and Powell dead, and his former boss, Confederate Secretary of State Judah Benjamin, having escaped to England.*

---

* The Confederate officials associated with the Canadian venture are on record with vehement denials of knowledge concerning any plot against the President. Their outrage appears to be a reflection of honest emotion—and we are once again left pondering the question of men with official standing muttering oaths which, when they've been carried into action, are

Out of two trials filled with kangaroo justice, perjury, withheld evidence and prejudiced juries nevertheless comes loud and clear overwhelming evidence that three men—Booth, Powell, and Surratt—possessed the ability and skills, between them, to do such a deed. But only if they were acting in concert.

Of these three, only two—Powell and Surratt—are professionals at their bloody business. John Wilkes Booth's contribution to the deed was his loyalty to the South and his fame, which would gain him entrance to the President whether Lincoln was at the theatre or in his own executive office.

Most damning of all the evidence pointing to Surratt's ruthlessness is his lack of action regarding the execution of his mother. If he had been innocent, he would have lost nothing in coming to her defense. Note also that in his escape he was given all of the assistance reserved for important former Confederates—as if his presence at the mother's trial would not only forfeit his own life but perhaps endanger others' lives as well.

WITHIN THE CONTEXT OF A REPUBLIC, at least in theory, there should be no need for assassination. It is true that it is a lawless act anywhere, and therefore a crime, but it is not so simple a crime as, for example, murder. Assassination is the removal from office, by means of murder, of a political figure, and that puts it on the level of being a political act. Certainly few persons in America would have advocated putting Von Stauffenberg on trial for his life had his attempted assassination of Adolf Hitler been a success. In a dictatorship, or in a monarchy, or in any system not intrinsically responsive to the rule of the people, assassination can be—and has been—viewed as at least a necessary and valid political act. Viewed in this light,

---

remembered as never having been meant as orders. This is particularly true of Thompson, who—it will be recalled—had been relieved of his official role long before the assassination.

it is not an act directed at the man but, rather, a required action undertaken to achieve political ends.

It is also, in that sense, a concept that is antithetical to a Republic. So long as the democratic processes are working, political ends may be achieved by means far less cruel and drastic than murder—and, in fact, each voting American citizen has the opportunity every four years to achieve the same political end that assassination achieves. Assassination as a political act, in the United States or any other democracy, is not considered necessary—and it is therefore a very easy step to assume that when it happens it is the witless and useless act of a madman.

To admit otherwise would require the implied admission that the murdered President was not responsive to democratic institutions and principles. To say that an American President would be assassinated to achieve political ends would seem to require, as an example, that the President in question was ruling only with the support of a militarily powerful minority of the people, and requiring the majority by force of arms to submit to that minority-authority. It is small wonder that the American people cannot accept such requirements.

Such was the situation, however, during the period when Abraham Lincoln ruled as a President twice elected by a minority of his countrymen and commanding the nation by military rule. In the spring of 1865, as Lincoln took the oath of office following that second election, eleven states of the nation lay economically and politically destroyed in the most bloody war of American history. In the four years of Abraham Lincoln's administration, almost as many Americans died on battlefields as in all of the other wars of our history put together, and shortly after the war the state of Mississippi, to choose one example, spent 20 percent of its total annual income on artificial limbs. In newspapers North and South, the man in the White House was commonly called "the gorilla," and along with his chief general, "the butcher." In the North itself newspapers had been closed down and the right to a writ of habeas corpus suspended. Rioting against the draft in New York City in 1863 had been brutally suppressed, and military rule was common in many areas of wavering loyalty to the Washington government.

No amount of post-martyrdom mythology can obscure the essential fact that Abraham Lincoln, no matter how humane or wise or compassionate, was in Southern eyes a minority chief of state ruling by the bayonet.

Against the notion of Lincoln as the American Messiah pushes the fact of Abraham Lincoln the consummate and canny and wily politician, functioning with adroit and cunning maneuvers to hold together a shaky base of political power. He is the most classic target for assassination as a cold political act—the political figure whose removal will bring about immediate political change.

Finally, in the tragic timing of his death—in the news of the brutal murder on Good Friday coming within days of the victory he had promised for so long—it was a natural reaction for his very real humanity and compassion to be blown so large as to obscure the fact that he was—though our greatest President —only a man, and a political man at that.

As hindsight pitted the pettinesses of his detractors against the life of the man himself, it became a part of our history that no sane man could murder such a leader as this. He became, with Washington, our spiritual founder; more than a President, more than a man who had to stand for election and collect by fair means or foul a majority in the electoral college, more than a man who fumbled about for two disastrous years in search of a military strategist equal to the talents of his opponents, more than a human being with chronic stomach trouble and government-crippling bouts of melancholia.

And as the symbol of Good Father Abraham grew more and more firm with us, so did the assumption that only a madman would destroy him. As Caesar had his Brutus, as Jesus had his

Judas, so would Lincoln have his betrayer—thus did we create the scene of the crazed and demented actor, overcome with hate and dreams of glory, lashing out insanely against the man everyone else knew to be the Savior of the Union.*

And so, today Wilkes Booth's body lies in an unmarked grave in Baltimore. The bodies of Thomas Jefferson and his peers rest undisturbed under a twain of ground; Washington and his wife lie inside marble coffins above the ground, as do the Grants. The Lincoln family—his wife and his children—are all buried above ground in his tomb in Springfield. But the President himself sleeps under the protection of twelve feet of steel mesh and concrete, like a national talisman—the only body among our history's heroes around which we've felt constrained to construct a vault.

THE FACT REMAINS that the story of why Abraham Lincoln was murdered can only be completed within the confines of the Confederate cabal in Canada, modified with the understanding that men who are making history do not have the facts or the time available to historians, and may therefore act less rationally in making their decisions than contemporary reflection can comprehend. Particularly in times of chaos, men may act according to what they believe at the moment to be true, and if later events prove them to have been wrong in their assumptions, that is of little moment in understanding why they did what they did. At some point, history must be the study of actions undertaken because of what contemporary men in extraordinary circumstances believed to be fact.

There is a story told of Napoleon being approached by one of his officers inquiring what to do with a body of prisoners. Wracked by a sudden cough, the French Emperor hacked out, "*Ma sacre cou,*" whereupon the officer departed to carry out

---

* It is not overstatement that if insanity was defined—during Lincoln's administration—as failure to adore, or even respect, him, many Northerners would have deserved such a diagnosis.

the orders he had mistakenly heard given: "*Massacre tout.*"

Is it so difficult, for those of us in need of an ordered world, to understand the irrationalities of men functioning within the context of their dying nation and their wilted hopes? Our histories demand order, but our future by definition is chaotic. Was it not so, as well, in the past?

Wilkes Booth believed Lincoln to be a tyrant—and so did Powell, and so did Surratt. The fact that John Wilkes Booth occupies an unmarked spot in his family's burial plot at Baltimore's Greenmount Cemetery does not lessen the likelihood that had he murdered George III instead we would erect monuments to his memory.

THERE IS A LEGEND of an early nineteenth-century Indian chieftain—war-weary and perhaps with no other weapons left to his use—who placed a curse upon the United States government that was hungrily gobbling up his lands and the lands of all his brothers. Each President of the United States, according to the curse, who had the misfortune to enter office in a year ending with zero would not leave that office alive.

So it has happened, since 1820.

That is eight Presidents dead in the White House—four of them the victims of an assassin's bullet. To understand the first of these, in particular, requires viewing his death within the turbulent context of the half-decade of near anarchy through which he led us, and—perhaps most importantly of all—to separate facts from the mythology surrounding him and his times, a mythology that has led us to believe no one but a madman could murder a leader so wise, so good, so humane and decent, as Abraham Lincoln.

For the overwhelming weight of the evidence points to the existence of a plot to kill him, a desperate last attempt by desperate and isolated men to gain independence for their Confederacy, and while the advantage of hindsight may cause some to see it as a totally absurd plot doomed obviously to failure, the fact nevertheless serves only to make the success of it so much more tragic.

And yet, even as we are drawn to Indian curses or some other equally insubstantial mythologies to explain the deaths of martyrs, still we must all insist upon recalling Cassius' more valid explanation of the assassination of Caesar:

"The fault, dear Brutus, is not in our stars, but in ourselves."

BIBLIOGRAPHY

A Legal View of the Seizure of Messrs. Mason and Slidell, New York, 1861.
ADAMS, Charles Francis: *The Crisis of Foreign Intervention in the War of Secession. September–November, 1862.* Massachusetts Historical Society, Boston, 1914.
ADAMS, Ephraim Douglass: *Great Britain and the American Civil War.* Vols. I and II. Longmans, Green & Co., New York, 1925.
ANGLE, Paul M., ed.: *A Portrait of Abraham Lincoln in Letters by His Oldest Son.* The Chicago Historical Society, Chicago, 1968.
AYER, I. Winslow: *The Great North-Western Conspiracy in All Its Startling Details.* James R. Walsh, Baldwin & Bamford, Chicago, 1865.
BAILEY, Thomas A.: *Presidential Greatness.* Appleton-Century, New York, 1966.
BARTHOLOMEW, Paul C.: *Summaries of Leading Cases on the Constitution.* Littlefield, Adams & Co., New Jersey, 1961.
BASLER, Roy P., ed.: *The Collected Works of Abraham Lincoln.* Rutgers University Press, New Brunswick, New Jersey, 1953. Index, Vol. I (1824–1848), Vol. II (1848–1858), Vol. III (1858–1860), Vol. IV (1860–1861), Vol. V (1861–1862), Vol. VI (1862–1863), Vol. VII (1863–1864), Vol. VIII (1864–1865).
BASLER, Roy P., ed.: *The Collected Works of Abraham Lincoln,* Supplement 1832–1865. Greenwood Press, Westport, Connecticut, 1974.
BEALE, Howard K., ed.: *Diary of Gideon Wells,* Secretary of the Navy Under Lincoln and Johnson, Vol. III (Jan. 1, 1867–June 6, 1869). W. W. Norton & Co., Inc., New York, 1960.
BERKY, Andrew S., and SHENTON, James P.: *The Historians' History of the United States,* Vols. I and II. G. P. Putnam's Sons, New York, 1966.
BERNSTEIN, Barton J., ed.: *Towards a New Past: Dissenting Essays in American History.* Vintage Books, New York, 1969.
BIGELOW, John: *France and the Confederate Navy (1862–1868).* Bergman Publishers, New York, 1968.
BINNEY, Horace: *The Privilege of the Writ of Habeas Corpus*

Under The Constitution. C. Sherman & Sons, Printer, Philadelphia, 1862.
BLAINE, James G.: *Twenty Years of Congress: From Lincoln to Garfield With a Review of the Events Which Led to the Political Revolution of 1860.* Vols. I and II. The Henry Bill Publishing Company, Norwalk, Connecticut, 1884.
BROOKS, Noah: *Washington in Lincoln's Time.* Holt, Rinehart and Winston, Inc., New York, 1958.
BUCHANAN, Lamont: *A Pictorial History of the Confederacy.* Crown Publishers, Inc., New York, 1961.
CALLAHAN, James Morton: *The Diplomatic History of the Southern Confederacy.* Greenwood Press, New York, 1968.
CANBY, Courtlandt, ed.: *Lincoln and the Civil War.* Dell Publishing Co., Inc., New York, 1958.
CARMAN, Harry J., and LUTHIN, Reinhard H.: *Lincoln and the Patronage.* Columbia University Press, New York, 1943.
CARR, Robert K., BERNSTEIN, Marver H., MORRISON, Donald H., and McLEAN, Joseph E.: *American Democracy in Theory and Practice,* 3rd ed. Holt, Rinehart and Winston, Inc., New York, 1959.
CHARNWOOD, Lord: *Abraham Lincoln.* Garden City Publishing Co., Inc., Garden City, New York, 1917.
CHUTE, William P., ed.: *The American Scene: 1860 to the Present, Contemporary Views of Life and Society.* Bantam Books, New York, 1966.
CLARKE, Asia Booth: *The Unlocked Book.* Faber & Faber, London, 1938.
COIT, Margaret L.: *John C. Calhoun, American Portrait.* Houghton Mifflin Company, Boston, 1950.
CONGRESSIONAL GLOBE, The, Supplement to: *The Proceedings of the Senate Sitting for the Trial of Andrew Johnson, Fortieth Congress, Second Session.* Published by F. and J. Rives and George A. Bailey, reporters and printers of the debates of Congress, Washington City, 1868.
COTTRELL, John: *Anatomy of an Assassination.* Frederick Muller, Ltd., Great Britain, 1966.
CULLOP, Charles P.: *Confederate Propaganda in Europe, 1861–1865.* University of Miami Press, Coral Gables, Florida, 1969.
DAILY NATIONAL INTELLIGENCER, January 1, 1865, thru June 30, 1865. Reel No. 108, Reproduction by the Library of Congress Photoduplication Service.
DANA, Charles A.: *Recollections of the Civil War.* Collier Books, New York, 1963.
DAVIS, Jefferson: *The Rise and Fall of the Confederate Government,* Vol. I. Thomas Yoseloff, Publisher, South Brunswick, 1958.
DENNETT, Tyler, ed.: *Lincoln and the Civil War in the Diaries*

and Letters of John Hay. Dodd, Mead & Co., New York, 1939.
DIX, Morgan, ed.: *Memoirs of John Adams Dix*, Vol. II. Harper & Brothers, New York, 1883.
DONALD, Aida DiPace and DONALD, David, ed.: *Diary of Charles Francis Adams*, Vol. I (Jan. 1820–June 1825). Belknap Press, Cambridge, Mass., 1964.
DONALD, David: *Charles Sumner and the Coming of the Civil War*. Alfred A. Knopf, New York, 1961.
DOWDEY, Clifford: *The Land They Fought For; The Story of the South As the Confederacy, 1832–1865*. Doubleday & Company, Inc., Garden City, New York, 1955.
DOWDEY, Clifford: *The Seven Days: The Emergence of Lee*. Little, Brown and Company, Boston, 1964.
DOWDEY, Clifford, ed.: *The Wartime Papers of R. E. Lee*. Little, Brown and Company, Boston, 1961.
DOWNER, Edward T.: *Stonewall Jackson's Shenandoah Valley Campaign, 1862*. Published by Stonewall Jackson Memorial Incorporated, Lexington, Virginia, 1959.
DUBERMAN, Martin B.: *Charles Francis Adams, 1807–1886*. Houghton Mifflin Co., Boston, 1961.
EISENSCHIML, Otto: *Why Was Lincoln Murdered?* Grosset & Dunlap, New York, 1937.
ELLIS, C. M.: *The Power of the Commander-In-Chief to Declare Martial Law, and Decree Emancipation: as shown from B. R. Curtis*. A. Williams & Co., Boston, 1862.
EVENING STAR, The: December 20, 1864, thru July 24, 1865. Reproduction by the Library of Congress Photoduplication Service.
FIELD, E. W.: *Correspondence on the Present Relations Between Great Britain and the U. S. of A*. Little, Brown & Co., Boston, 1862.
FOOTE, Shelby: *The Civil War, A Narrative: Fort Sumter to Perryville*. Random House, New York, 1958.
FOOTE, Shelby: *The Civil War, A Narrative: Fredericksburg to Meridian*. Random House, New York, 1963.
FREDERICKS, Pierce G., ed.: *The Civil War As They Knew It*. Bantam Books, New York, 1961.
FREEMAN, Douglass Southall: *Lee's Lieutenants: A Study in Command*, Vol. I, Manassas to Malvern Hill. Chas. Scribner's Sons, New York, 1942.
FREEMAN, Douglass Southall: *Lee's Lieutenants: A Study in Command*, Vol. II, Cedar Mountain to Chancellorsville. Chas. Scribner's Sons, New York, 1943.
FREEMAN, Douglass Southall: *Lee's Lieutenants: A Study in Command*, Vol. III, Gettysburg to Appomattox. Chas. Scribner's Sons, New York, 1944.
FREEMAN, Douglass Southall: *R. E. Lee, A Biography*, Vol. I. Chas. Scribner's Sons, New York, 1934.

GRANT, U. S.: *Personal Memoirs of U. S. Grant*, Vol. I and II. Charles L. Webster & Company, New York, 1886.
GRAY, Wood: *The Hidden Civil War: The Story of the Copperheads*. Viking Press, New York, 1942.
GRIERSON, Francis: *The Valley of Shadows, The Coming of the Civil War in Lincoln's Midwest: A Contemporary Account*. Harper & Row, New York, 1948.
GURLEY, Dr.: *Sermon at the Funeral of Abraham Lincoln: Faith in God*. Department of History, Presbyterian Church, Philadelphia, 1940.
HARRIS, Thomas L.: *The Trent Affair: Review of English and American Relations at the Beginning of the Civil War*. The Bowen-Merrill Company, Indianapolis and Kansas City, 1896.
HASKELL, Frank A.: *The Battle of Gettysburg*. Houghton Mifflin Company, Boston, 1958.
HEFFNER, Richard D.: *A Documentary History of the United States*. Mentor Book, New American Library, New York, 1963.
HENDERSON, Colonel G. F. R.: *Stonewall Jackson and the American Civil War*. David McKay, New York, 1961.
HENDRICK, Burton J.: *Lincoln's War Cabinet*. Dolphin Books, Garden City, New York, 1961.
HERNDON, William H., and WEIK, Jesse W.: *Abraham Lincoln: The True Story of a Great Life*, Vols. I and II. D. Appleton and Company, New York, 1893.
HESSELTINE, William B.: *Lincoln's Plan of Reconstruction*. Peter Smith, Publisher, Gloucester, Mass., 1963.
HILL, Daniel Harvey: *Hal Bridges, Lee's Maverick General*. McGraw-Hill Book Company, Inc., New York, 1961.
HORAN, James D.: *Confederate Agent: A Discovery in History*. Crown Publishers, Inc., New York, 1954.
HORNER, Harlan Hoyt: *Lincoln and Greeley*. University of Illinois Press, 1953.
HURD, Charles, and HURD, Eleanor, ed.: *A Treasury of Great American Letters*. Hawthorn Books, Inc., New York, 1961.
JOHNSON, Angus James II: *Virginia Railroads in the Civil War*. The University of North Carolina Press, Chapel Hill, 1961.
JORDAN, Donaldson, and PRATT, Edwin J.: *Europe and the American Civil War*. Houghton Mifflin Company, Boston and New York, The Riverside Press, Cambridge, 1931.
KELLER, Morton: *The Art and Politics of Thomas Nash*. Oxford University Press, New York, 1968.
KELLY, Edward James: *The Assassination of Abraham Lincoln: The Crime at Ford's Theatre*. Action Publications, Alexandria, Virginia, 1944.
KIMMEL, Stanley: *The Mad Booths of Maryland*, Bobbs-Merrill Co., New York, 1940.

KLEMENT, Frank L.: *The Copperheads in the Middle West.* University of Chicago Press, 1960.
KUNHARDT, Dorothy Meserve, and KUNHARDT, Philip B., Jr.: *Twenty Days.* Castle Books, New York, 1965.
LAMON, Ward Hill: *Recollections of Abraham Lincoln, 1847–1865*, Dorothy Lamon Teillard, ed. Published by the editor, Washington, 1911.
LEWIS, Lloyd: *Myths After Lincoln.* Blue Ribbon Books, Inc., New York, 1929.
LIEUTENANT COLONEL ——: *John Yates Beall, The Pirate Spy.* T. R. Dawley, New York, 1865.
LONGSTREET, James: *From Manassas to Appomattox*, edited with introduction and notes by James I. Robertson, Jr. Indiana University Press, Bloomington, Indiana, 1969.
LORANT, Stefan: *Lincoln, His Life in Photographs.* Duell, Sloan and Pearce, New York, 1941.
LOSSING, Benson J.: *Our Country. A Household History for All Readers, from the Discovery of America to the Present Time*, in three volumes. Henry J. Johnson, New York, 1878.
LOWREY, G. P.: *English Neutrality: Is the "Alabama" a British Pirate?* Anson D. F. Randolph, New York, 1863.
LUCAS, Daniel B.: *Memoirs of John Yates Beall.* Printed by J. Lovell, Montreal, 1865.
McBRIDE, Robert W.: *Personal Recollections of Abraham Lincoln.* The Bobbs-Merrill Co., Indianapolis, 1926.
McCARTHY, Charles H.: *Lincoln's Plan of Reconstruction.* AMS Press, Inc., New York, 1966.
McCLELLAN, George B.: *McClellan's Own Story—A War for the Union.* Charles L. Webster & Company, New York, 1887.
MASTERS, Roger D.: *The Nation Is Burdened.* Alfred A. Knopf, New York, 1957.
MEADE, Robert D.: *Judah P. Benjamin, Confederate Statesman.* Oxford University Press, London, 1943.
MERLI, Frank J.: *Great Britain and the Confederate Navy. 1861–1865.* Indiana University Press, 1965.
MESERVE, Frederick Hill, and SANDBURG, Carl: *The Photographs of Abraham Lincoln and the Face of Lincoln.* Harcourt, Brace & Co., Inc., New York, 1944.
MILTON, George Fort: *Abraham Lincoln and The Fifth Column.* The Vanguard Press, New York, 1942.
MITCHELL, Lt. Col. Joseph B.: *Decisive Battles of the Civil War.* Fawcett Publications, Inc., Greenwich, Connecticut, 1962.
MITGANG, Herbert, ed.: *Lincoln As They Saw Him.* Holt, Rinehart and Winston, New York and Toronto, 1965.
MOORE, Guy W.: *The Case of Mrs. Surratt: Her Controversial Trial and Execution for Conspiracy in the Lincoln Assassination.*

The University of Oklahoma Press, Norman, Oklahoma, 1954.
MORISON, Samuel Eliot: *The Oxford History of the American People*. Oxford University Press, New York, 1965.
MUZZEY, David Saville: *History of the American People*. Ginn and Company, Boston, 1929.
MUZZEY, David Saville: *Readings in American History*. Ginn and Company, Boston, 1915.
NEVINS, Allan: *A Diary of Battle; The Personal Journals of Colonel Charles S. Wainwright, 1861–1865*. Harcourt, Brace & World, New York, 1962.
NICHOLS, Jeannette P., and NICHOLS, Roy F.: *The Growth of American Democracy*. D. Appleton-Century Company, Inc., New York, 1939.
NICOLAY, John G.: *A Short Life of Abraham Lincoln*, condensed from Nicolay and Hay's *Abraham Lincoln: A History*. The Century Co., New York, 1902.
NICOLAY, John G., and HAY, John, eds.: *Complete Works of Abraham Lincoln*, Vols. I through XII. The Lamb Publishing Co., New York, 1894.
OWLS-GLASS: *Rebel Brag and British Bluster*. The American News Company, 1865.
PEASE, Theodore Calvin, ed.: *The Diary of Orville Hickman*. The Trustees of the Illinois State Historical Library, Springfield, Illinois, 1925.
PHILLIPS, Ulrich Bonnell: *Life and Labor in the Old South*. Grosset & Dunlap, New York, 1929.
PIERCE, Edward L.: *Memoir and Letters of Charles Sumner*, Vol. III, 1845–1860. Roberts Brothers, Publishers, Boston, 1893.
PITMAN, Benn: *The Assassination of President Lincoln and the Trial of the Conspirators*. Greenwood Press, Westport, Connecticut, 1974.
PLOWDEN, David: *Lincoln and His America 1809–1865*. Viking Press, New York, 1970.
POLLEY, Robert L., ed.: *Lincoln, His Words and His World*. Country Beautiful Foundation, Inc., Waukesha, Wisconsin, for Hawthorn Books, Inc., New York, 1965.
POTTER, David M.: *Lincoln and His Party in the Secession Crisis*. Yale University Press, New Haven, Connecticut, 1942.
RANDALL, J. G., and DONALD, David: *The Civil War and Reconstruction*. D. C. Heath and Company, Boston, 1961.
RANKIN, Henry B.: *Personal Recollections of Abraham Lincoln*. G. P. Putnam's Sons/The Knickerbocker Press, New York & London, 1916.
REED, William Bradford: *A Review of Mr. Seward's Diplomacy by A Northern Man*. A pamphlet, no identification.

REPORTER, The: *The Trial of John H. Surratt*, V. 3, pp. 57–405, and V. 4, *The Reporter*. Washington, D.C., 1867.
RICE, Allen Thorndike: *Reminiscences of Abraham Lincoln by Distinguished Men of His Time*. North American Publishing Co., New York, 1886.
ROBERTSON, James I., Jr.: *Civil War History*. Vol. VII, State University of Iowa, 1961.
ROSCOE, Theodore: *The Lincoln Assassination, April 14, 1865*. Franklin Watts, Inc., New York, 1971.
SANDBURG, Carl: *Abraham Lincoln* (in three volumes). Laurel Edition, Dell Publishing Co., Inc., New York, 1960.
SARGENT, F. W.: *England, the United States, and The Southern Confederacy*. Negro Universities Press, a Division of the Greenwood Press, Inc., New York, 1969.
SCOTT, John A.: *Living Documents in American History*. Washington Square Press, Inc., New York, 1964.
SEARCHER, Victor: *The Farewell to Lincoln*. Abingdon Press, New York, 1965.
SEGAL, Charles M., ed.: *Conversations With Lincoln*. G. P. Putnam's Sons, New York, 1961.
SEMMES, Raphael: *The Confederate Raider Alabama*. Fawcett Publications, Inc., Greenwich, Connecticut, 1962.
SHAKESPEARE, William: *The Tragedy of Macbeth*. Edited by Eugene M. Waith. Yale University Press, New Haven, Connecticut, 1966.
SHELTON, Vaughan: *Mask for Treason—The Lincoln Murder Trial*. Stackpole Books, Harrisburg, Pa., 1965.
SHERIDAN, P. H.: *Personal Memoirs of P. H. Sheridan, General United States Army*, Vols. I & II. Charles L. Webster & Company, New York, 1888.
SIDEMAN, Belle Becker, and FRIEDMAN, Lillian, eds.: *Europe Looks at the Civil War*. Collier Books, New York, 1962.
SILBER, Irwin, ed.: *Songs of the Civil War*. Columbia University Press, New York, 1960.
SMITH, George Winston, and JUDAH, Charles: *Life in the North During the Civil War*. The University of New Mexico Press, Albuquerque, N. M., 1966.
The Statistical History of the United States from Colonial Times to the Present. Fairfield Publishers, Inc., Stanford, Connecticut.
STAUDENRAUS, P. J., ed.: *Mr. Lincoln's Washington: Selections from the Writings of Noah Brooks, Civil War Correspondent*. Thomas Yoseloff, Publisher, New York and London, 1967.
STEARN, Gerald Emanuel, and FRIED, Albert, eds.: *The Essential Lincoln*. Collier Books, New York, 1962.

STERN, Philip Van Doren: *The Man Who Killed Lincoln*. Dell Publishing Company, New York, 1955.
STRACHEY, Lytton: *Queen Victoria*. Harcourt, Brace and Company, New York, 1921.
SUMNER, Charles: *Speech of Hon. Charles Sumner Before the Citizens of New York at Cooper Institute, September 10, 1863*. Wm. V. Spencer, publisher, Wright & Potter, printers, Boston, 1863.
THOMAS, Benjamin P., and HYMAN, Harold M.: *Stanton: The Life and Times of Lincoln's Secretary of War*. Alfred A. Knopf, New York, 1962.
UNITED STATES ADJUTANT GENERAL'S OFFICE, MILITARY COMMISSION: *Trial of John Yates Beall*. D. Appleton & Co., New York, 1865.
VALLANDIGHAM, Rev. James L.: *A Life of Clement L. Vallandigham*. Turnbull Brothers, Baltimore, 1872.
VILLIERS, Broughain and CHESSON, W. H.: *Anglo-American Relations, 1861–1865*. Charles Scribner's Sons, New York, 1920.
WARE, Captain Eugene F.: *The Indian War of 1864*. St. Martin's Press, New York, 1960.
WARREN, Charles: *The Supreme Court in United States History*, two volumes. Little, Brown and Company, Boston, 1926.
WATKINS, Sam R.: "*Co. Aytch*." Collier Books, New York, 1962.
WAUGH, Edgar Wiggins: *Second Consul*. Bobbs-Merrill Company, Inc., Indianapolis, 1956.
WEICHMANN, Louis J.: *A True History of the Assassination of Abraham Lincoln and of the Conspiracy of 1865*, edited by Floyd E. Risvold. Alfred A. Knopf, New York, 1975.
WELLMAN, Paul I.: *Glory, God and Gold*. Doubleday & Company, Inc., Garden City, New York, 1954.
WERSTEIN, Irving: *July 1863*. Ace Books, New York, 1957.
WHEELER, Kenneth W.: *For the Union/Ohio Leaders in the Civil War*. Ohio State University Press, 1968.
WILLIAMS, Harry T.: *Lincoln and the Radicals*. The University of Wisconsin Press, 1965.
WILSON, Rufus Rockwell: *Intimate Memories of Lincoln*. The Primavera Press, Inc., Elmira, N.Y., 1945.
WINKS, Robin W.: *Canada and the United States–The Civil War Years*. The Johns Hopkins Press, Baltimore, 1960.
WIRTH, Conrad L.: *Restoration of Ford's Theatre* (Historic Structures Report). U.S. Department of the Interior publication, 1963.
WOODWARD, W. E.: *Meet General Grant*. The Sun Dial Press, New York, 1928.

NOTES

THESE BRIEF NOTES are meant to point out the more important sources utilized in preparation of the chapters, and to note certain information which I was reluctant to have interrupt the main flow of the narrative. The reader should understand that any book about a single phase in history is only a part of a whole, only an advocacy —only, for that matter, a phrase in a language. This has been a book about an assassination conspiracy; it has by necessity omitted much that is necessary to understanding the mid-nineteenth century in America and in Europe. Further, distilling fact from fiction in the Lincoln Conspiracy is a laborious—and controversial—task. These notes, then, are meant to draw the reader's attention to those sources and resources which I believe should be read in their entirety, and to cover those controversial grounds that I did not identify as such in the narrative itself.

Chapter I: Introduction to the Play

A *sanglot* is, in translation from the French, literally a choke or a sob. It refers to the practice, in music, of intentionally breaking a single note to mimic a human sob. There is some disagreement as to whether or not Laura Keene actually cradled Lincoln's head in her lap, as I've described her doing. However, many accounts have her doing so, and there is a purported piece of her gown, appropriately bloodstained, in an Ohio museum. The description of the military maneuvers which might have followed Lincoln's assassin's successful flight to Canada is based upon the actual positions and objectives of each command and each nation that is mentioned.

Chapter II: North of the North

Two complex subjects—the election of 1864 and the "Great Northwest Conspiracy"—are dealt with in condensed form to provide the reader with a necessary background for understanding the main theme of the book, but these condensations are by no means intended to provide a full picture of either of those two subjects.

The reader without access to a large library will have difficulty finding works on the Northwest Conspiracy, but *The Collected Works of Abraham Lincoln, Stanton: The Life and Times of Lincoln's Secretary of War,* and *Lincoln's War Cabinet*—all of which are listed in the bibliography—provide a decent basic background to the politics of the period and are available through most libraries.

Chapter III: Border Incidents

Sadly, there are few texts generally available treating upon the relations between Canada and the United States during the Civil War. Several cover foreign relations in general, however, and the reader is directed to any of the bibliography's listings which can be found in his or her bookstores and libraries—particularly, *Canada and the United States: The Civil War Years.*

Chapter IV: "Wilkes Booth Came to Washington . . ."

The best account of the Booth family is *The Mad Booths of Maryland,* but for a clearer understanding of Wilkes this book should be read only in company with his sister's memoir, *The Unlocked Book.* Other than the biographical passages, all of the quotations used in this chapter are from Benn Pitman's official record of the trial of the conspirators. A disputable statement of fact in the chapter involves my placing Lincoln in the audience for Booth's performance in *The Marble Heart.* There is little hard evidence that the President attended this performance, but I am personally inclined to believe, in the absence of evidence to the contrary, the little evidence that he was there.

Chapter V: A Small Company of Irregulars

This chapter relies heavily upon the memories of witnesses at the conspiracy trial, Charles A. Dana, and Asia Booth Clarke. The attempt or attempts at kidnapping Lincoln which Surratt, Booth and the others are frequently held to have spent months scheming over are only slightly documented—the only action taken in the conspiracy appears to be the one which culminated in Salmon P. Chase's being accosted by them. What they were really doing during this period is suggested in Asia's book, *The Unlocked Book,* regarding Wilkes' activities as a smuggler of quinine. Only Weichmann speaks of a continuing conspiracy against Lincoln, and the reader who is familiar with Weichmann's testimony and his posthumously published memoirs will note that I rely upon his truthfulness in some instances and regard him as a liar in others. As the narrative explains,

Weichmann was under intense pressure during the conspiracy trial, and after Mrs. Surratt was hanged, he spent the rest of his life as a pariah whose cowardice had sent her, unfairly, to the gallows. This latter is perhaps the most accurate—and what twenty-three-year-old boy could withstand a Stantonian threat of death unless his memory improved? By the same token, Weichmann is the only "insider" eyewitness who talked and wrote a lot—he is today, as he was then, the "key" witness. I've used a complex system for separating his truths from his embellished truths. First, where other witnesses were present and separately confirmed his statements, I've accepted his accounts. Second, where his accounts are corroborated by the subsequent actions of the principals, I've accepted his accounts. Third, where he discusses minor details that could lead to any conclusions, I've tended to believe his account. In other instances not passing these tests, I've assumed he is lying or embellishing—and in many cases with Weichmann it is an embellishment, a slight bit of interpretation of what he saw, such as when he gave the testimony which sent the innocent Mary Surratt to the hangman. He saw her talk with her tenant on the Maryland farm, and—later—assumed it was conspiracy talk. There is no doubt in my mind that Weichmann in his testimony—and even more strongly in his memoirs—grew to believe that what he had witnessed was part of the conspiracy the government tried to prove.

Chapter VI: The Last Days of the Lost Cause

One quotation attributed in this chapter regarding Beall comes from Carl Sandburg, and I've not been able to find supporting primary sources. All other quotations have either primary or multiple sources. The involvement of Beall, by the way, includes rumors which have been taught from generation to generation in the Old Virginia families that Booth was in love with Beall's sister and had been a schoolmate of the young Confederate officer. This is poppycock. Some accounts say that Booth himself, on bended knee, pleaded with the President for Beall's life, and then killed Lincoln to avenge Beall's own death. The stories, of course, are ridiculous—but simply by linking the two men they support previous evidence that, given the distortions of rumor, there was indeed a link between them through Montreal.

Chapter VII: The Ultimate Border Incident

Frustratingly little is documented about John Surratt's journey from Richmond to Montreal, as described in this chapter. What is known is here. The possible involvement of Jefferson Davis or of Judah Benjamin in the assassination is not addressed in the narrative because, lacking hard evidence, I must end the tracing of the assassination concept with Surratt.

Chapter VIII: "Long Live Our Chief, the President..."

Virtually all information in this chapter is derived from the two trial transcripts. The major disputable point involves the question of whether or not Booth prepared the bar for the outer door of the box and bored a hole in the door to Lincoln's box. In response to a letter from me in 1965, Mr. Frank A. Ford wrote the following:

> Thank you, Mr. Starkey, for your letter of the 13th asking for more information concerning "who bored the hole" and other questions you raise. Sorry but I do not know who did the actual boring. I suppose it was done by the stage carpenter or one of the stage hands. Secondly: While Booth did have access to the theatre (they called it "professional courtesy" in those days), getting mail there and visiting actors, he did not have freedom to bore holes in and prepare bars for theatre doors. I assume you do not know that the locks to the doors of the boxes did not function. Keys to the same were mislaid or lost. Thus, such makeshift "locksmithing" was to insure privacy and the hole was bored for a "looksee."

In this chapter, I've portrayed the guard, Parker, as standing carefully at his post until the famous actor Wilkes Booth approaches and asks permission to enter, offering his card, as eyewitnesses saw him do. The common assumption is that Parker left his post, and in that same letter Mr. Ford agrees, though denying expertise: "I do not know Parker's reason for leaving his post. Investigation never touched on that but no doubt your assumption could be correct. For my part I think the poor unfortunate misfit just wanted to see the performance from the dress circle. I hope I have helped you. I know only what my father told me years after when the myth about the hole came to light, through many publications, etc., and so many believed it with dozens of other myths such as the one 'they never caught Booth.'" All that is really documented about Parker is that he was seen on duty outside the box before the murder, and was seen after it the next morning when he brought a prostitute he'd arrested into the police station. No one saw him leave his post. No one ever testified to seeing him in the dress circle. At least two eyewitnesses, both quoted in this chapter, saw him admit someone, upon presentation of a calling card. Again, I do not believe the legends above the evidence—Parker remained at his post, passed the famous actor after he presented his card, and then, out of a sense of guilt and remorse and perhaps even self-serving stupidity, showed up with an arrested whore to prove he was a good cop.

Chapter IX: The Secretary's Medicine

In this chapter, I describe Secretary Seward as a passive figure during the attack, and then quote Mrs. Seward saying he interposed himself between Fanny, his daughter, and the assassin to protect her. Mrs. Seward should be forgiven for seeing her prostrate husband as a hero; for my part, the idea of the object of the attack protecting a bystander—particularly when he was prostrate with pain—and doing so successfully without sacrificing his life is beyond belief, as well as being counter to eyewitness accounts. Mrs. Lincoln's grief was at least a grief of certainty, since her husband was dead; Mrs. Seward had to live for weeks with both a husband and a son at death's door. My account, therefore, expresses the fact; hers, in painful eloquence, is included to express the horror.

Chapter X: "Hail to the Chief..."

Almost all of the quotations are from trial testimony. The description of happenings in the Presidential Box is based upon several walk-throughs at Ford's Theatre since its reconstruction. Given the dimensions of the box and the positions of the participants, my account—though it differs with previous accounts—must be the accurate one, and is the only hindsight description written since the reconstruction of the box. There was simply no room for Booth to go behind Lincoln, and Rathbone would have to have been coming toward him from the rear of the box as Booth reached the center in order to be cut by Booth's knife in the manner Rathbone describes.

Chapter XI: The Midnight Special

The opening lines, set in italics, are fictional only in the sense that they have no source. All of what went before and followed after this scene requires that some such scene took place. The rest of the chapter follows trial testimony quotations. The train schedules are from contemporary newspaper advertisements, and the information on Booth's ability to ride from Surratt's Tavern to Baltimore comes from the trainer of a Kentucky Derby winner. It is buttressed by the fact that Booth, troubled with a broken leg, covered half that distance in making it to Dr. Mudd's house.

Chapter XII: Running Away on One Leg

All comments on Booth's diary are from a personal inspection of it and from the government transcript. Other sources of quotations are the trial transcripts, newspaper accounts, and the later memoirs of Jones. The account of Booth's suicide can be disputed—a reward, in fact, was paid to one Boston Corbett on his claim to have been the man who killed Booth. It is my very firm belief that Booth killed himself; the track of his wound was potentially self-inflicted, he swore he'd not be taken alive, and Corbett carried a rifle, while Booth's was a pistol wound.

Chapter XIII: The Missing Link

The serious reader seeking further information should find a copy of *Myths After Lincoln*, which is listed in the bibliography. The bulk of this chapter is based on *The Assassination of President Lincoln and the Trial of the Conspirators* by Benn Pitman.

Chapter XIV: Postmortem

The primary source for this chapter is John Surratt's own trial, the transcript of which is noted in the bibliography. But a warning: I believe Surratt to have been guilty, but the Black Republican hacks assembled as prosecutors and judge sufficiently slandered a valorous defense counsel that the jury—or a sufficient portion of it —rebelled. The transcript is fascinating, therefore, only to students of the law, or of history, and is predominantly filled with lawyer's arguments. Surratt's lawyer will not be surpassed in his profession for ethics or brilliance; the prosecution cannot be bettered for a lack of either, or for incompetence. It is my very strong opinion that a competent, rather than a political, prosecutor would have convicted Surratt. But the times were political rather than legal.

INDEX

Adams, Charles, 32–33
Alabama, C.S.A., 32
Anderson, Mary Jane, 93
Anderson, Major Robert, 88
Antietam, 32, 69
Arnold, Samuel, 57, 68, 152, 165
Atzerodt, George, 58, 138, 143, 153; assassination preparations, 91–92, 97–99, 100–101; conspiracy trial, 164, 165, 166, 176; ferryboat, 125, 127; plot to kidnap Lincoln, 68–70; set up as conspirator, 100–101, 121, 127, 133, 183

Bainbridge, A. S., 143
Baker, Lafayette, 146–148, 162, 175, 182
Barnes, Joseph K., U.S. Surgeon-General, 4–5, 110–112, 151
Barton, George D. F., U.S. Navy Paymaster, 169–170
Beall, John Yates, 37–41, 74–79
Bell, William, 106–107, 110
Benjamin, Judah P., C.S.A. Secretary of State, 10, 21, 24, 55, 57, 78, 81, 167–168, 178, 183
Blair, Montgomery, U.S. Postmaster-General, 75
Booth, Blanche de Bar, 47
Booth, Edwin, 44–46, 49, 51, 53–54, 134, 161
Booth, John Wilkes (alias John William Boyd): assassin, 6–7, 8–9, 59–60, 114–119, 161; assassination preparations, 89, 93, 96–101; career, 44, 47, 48–52, 54, 63–64, 66; conspiracy trial, 156, 158–159, 162–168, 176; early years, 45–47, 48; escape, 120–149, 151, 152, 153, 154, 170, 179; involvement with Canadian Confederates, 52, 55, 66, 86; involvement with Washington confederates, 53, 56–58, 59, 183, 184; plot to kidnap Lincoln, 67–71; political philosophy, 64–65, 136–137, 139, 174, 188
Booth, Junius Brutus, 45–46, 51, 134
Booth, Junius Brutus, Jr., 45–46, 53–54
Booth, Mary Ann Holmes, 45–46, 54
Boyd, John William, *see* Booth, John Wilkes
Brown, John, 64–65
Browning, Senator Orville H., 75–77, 79
Browning, William A., 92
Buchanan, James, 21, 153
Bulwar-Lytton, Sir Edward, 32
Burnside, General Ambrose E., 22, 87
Burroughs, Peanuts, 93, 98–99, 114, 119

Campbell, Archibald, 85
Canada: as Confederate base, 23, 25, 44, 52, 55, 68, 78, 80, 82, 83–84, 159, 166, 167; as prospective U.S. colony, 28–29, 34, 35–36, 168, 182–183; escape to,

9, 125–126, 151, 152, 155, 170, 177–178, 180; foreign policy, 76; plans to provoke war with, 10, 20–22; relations with U.S., 39, 40–41, 73–74
Capitol Building, 3, 15, 152
Chase, Salmon P., 70–71
Clay, Clement C., 21, 25, 158
Clarke, Asia Booth, 46–49, 63
Clarke, John Sleeper, 46, 49
Cleary, William C., 158
Cobb, Sgt. Silas, 122–123, 124, 125–127
Cole, Senator Cornelius, 61
Confederacy, 11–12, 17–18, 39, 66, 82–85, 104
Conger, Lieut. Col. Everton J., 147–148, 154, 162
Corbett, Boston, 147
Cox, Samuel, 131–133, 138

Dana, Charles A., U.S. Asst. Secretary of War, 27, 41–42, 61, 72–73, 82
Davis, Jefferson, 10, 15, 20–21, 26, 35, 66, 70, 75, 80–81, 82–84, 85, 86, 87, 153, 158–159, 162, 165–168, 183
Democratic party, 19, 23, 42
Dix, Major-General, John A., 40, 68, 73–75, 77
Dye, Sgt. Joseph M., 114–115

Emancipation Proclamation, 19, 32
Emerson, L. A., 113
England, *see* Great Britain
Enrica, see *Alabama*, C.S.A.
Evening Star (newspaper), 90

Ferguson, James P., 93, 118
Ferguson, W. J., 49
Fitzpatrick, Honora, 59
Fletcher, John, 99, 101
Ford, Dick, 90–91, 97
Ford, Harry, 90–91, 93–94, 95, 96, 97
Ford, John T., 89, 91, 94, 95–96

Ford's Theatre, 3–4, 5, 6, 8, 45, 52, 57, 63, 89–96, 105, 113–115, 125, 127, 152, 156, 179
Forrest, Edwin, 51
Fort Sumter, 31, 65, 88, 90
Fredericksburg, Va., 87, 88

Gardiner, Polk, 123
Garrett, Jack, 145
Garrett, Matt, 146
Garrett, Richard H., 128, 143, 144, 145–146
Garrett, William (Bill), 145, 154
Garrett's farm, 93, 127, 143–149, 154, 162, 182
Gettysburg, Pa., 18, 33, 34, 35, 69, 87–88
Gilbert, Mrs. G. H., 49
Grant, General Ulysses S., 11, 18, 33, 67–68, 70, 81–82, 87, 97, 104, 105, 159, 166, 187
Grant, Mrs. Ulysses S., 98, 105
Great Britain: foreign policy, 28, 29–31, 34–45, 39; plans to promote war against, 21, 27, 76; relations with the Confederacy, 73; relations with the Union, 105, 167, 171; treaties with U.S., 41, 77; Victoria, Queen, 31–32, 34, 36, 171
Great Northwest Conspiracy, 24, 27
Greeley, Horace, 25–26
Grover's Theatre, 48, 49, 89, 96–97

Hale, Lucy, 161
Harper, George, 158
Harris, Clara, 95
Harris, Brigadier General T. M., 157
Hawkes, Harry, 115, 116, 117
Herold, David E. (Davie), 58, 59–60; assassination preparations, 91, 97, 99, 100, 105, 124; conspiracy trial, 156, 164–167, 176; flight with Booth, 121, 123, 127, 129, 131–133, 137–138, 140, 142–147; 153; involvement with Seward, 106, 108, 110

Index

Herndon House, 92, 98
Hess, C. D., 89, 90
Holcombe, J. P., 21, 25
Holloway, Miss L. K. B., 144, 145
Holmes, Mary Ann, 45
Holt, Judge Advocate General Joseph, 157–158, 160–161, 168, 170, 173, 174
Howard's Stables, 92
Hunter, Major General David, 155, 156–157

Jett, Willie S., 143–146, 154, 162, 182
Johnson, Andrew, 5, 15, 19, 75, 91, 92, 98, 100, 101, 125, 127, 156, 159, 160, 165, 166, 172, 174, 175–176
Johnson, General Joseph E., 84–85, 87
Johnson, Reverdy, 160
Jones, Thomas A., 132–134, 136, 137–138
Juarez, Benito, 11

Keene, Laura, 4, 113, 135
Kelleher, James, 101
Kelleher's Stables, 92, 99–100
Kirkwood Hotel, 5, 15, 91, 98, 100, 101, 125, 127
Knights of the Golden Circle, The, 23

Lamon, Ward Hill, 62–63, 82
Leale, Dr. Charles, 4–5
Lee, General Robert E., 32, 37, 68, 79, 84–85, 87, 89, 104, 105
Lincoln, Abraham, 6, 8–11, 14, 16–20, 22, 23, 25–28, 41, 42, 44, 52, 55, 57, 59, 61–68, 70–78, 81, 82, 85, 86, 94–98, 102–105, 110, 112–114, 117, 118, 133, 134, 150–152, 154–156, 158–160, 162, 166–168, 172, 176, 177, 183–188
Lincoln, Mary Todd, 63, 81, 95, 98, 118, 119
Lincoln, Robert Todd, 81

Lincoln, Tad, 6, 15, 81
Lincoln, Willie, 153
Lloyd, John, 98, 123–124, 152, 155–156, 161, 163–164
London *Times*, 30, 74
Lucas, William, 140–142
Lyons, Lord Richard, 35, 40

Maddox, James, 93, 101
Manassas, 88
Manifest Destiny, 104
Matthews, John, 97, 136
Maximilian, 11
McClellan, General George Brinton, 17, 42
McCullough, 49
McGowan, Capt. Theodore, 116
Meade, General, C.S.A., 87
Mexico, 28, 29, 89
Michigan, U.S.S., 37, 38
Miles, John, 93
Monroe Doctrine, 28
Montgomery, Richard, 55
Morris, Clara, 50–51
Mosby, John S., 67, 69, 142
Mudd, Henry, 53
Mudd, Dr. Samuel A., 53, 56, 58, 60, 124, 127, 129, 131, 140, 151, 153, 156, 157, 164, 165; conspiracy trial of, 156–157, 164–165
Mudd, Mrs. Samuel A., 130

National Hotel, 44–45, 52–53, 55, 56, 97
National Intelligencer (newspaper), 97, 101, 134–135, 136–137
National Republican (newspaper), 90–91
National Theater, 93
Naylor's Stables, 91, 99
New York Herald, 54
New York Times, 39
New York Tribune, 25–26
New York World, 157

O'Laughlin, Michael, 57, 68, 152, 165

208 / Index

Order of American Knights, 23
Our American Cousin, 89, 115

Payne, Lewis, *see* Powell, Lewis
Parker, John, 113, 120
Peoria Convention, 24
Peyton, Lucy, 143
Peyton, Sarah Jane, 143
Philo Parsons, 36–38, 74
Port Royal, Va., 143, 145
Port Tobacco, Md., 58, 68, 125, 127, 133, 138
Porterfield, John, 42–43
Powell, Lewis Thornton (alias Payne or Wood), 58–59, 92, 152, 173, 182–183, 188; assassination preparations, 97, 98, 100; attack on Seward, 105–112, 122, 167; conspiracy trial, 156, 162–163, 165–166, 176, 184; plot to kidnap Lincoln, 68–70
Pumphrey, James, 96–97, 99, 101
Pumphrey's Livery Stable, 91, 96, 100

Queen, Dr., 53
Queen's Hotel, 12, 21, 42, 78, 79
Quesenberry, Mrs. Emma, 140

Rathbone, Major Henry R., 95, 118–119
Reed, David, 93
Robey, Franklin, 132
Robinson, George T., 105, 107–111
Ruggles, Mortimer B., 143
Rush-Bagot Agreement, 38–39, 41, 77
Russell, Lord John, 33

St. Albans, Vt., 39–41, 68, 74, 76, 126
Sangston, John, 179
Sanders, George, 158
Seward, Major Augustus, 105, 108, 109, 110, 111
Seward, Fanny, 104–105, 107–108, 109, 111

Seward, Frederick, U.S. Asst. Secretary of State, 105, 106–107 109, 110, 111
Seward, Mrs. Frederick, 111
Seward, William H., U.S. Secretary of State, attack on, 8, 58–59, 103–112, 124, 156, 159, 162–163, 166–167; diplomacy of, 28, 29–30, 31, 32, 35, 38, 41, 68, 76–77, 78, 171–172
Seward, Mrs. William H., 109, 111
Sheridan, General Philip, 81, 104
Sherman, General William T., 39, 84, 87
Simms, Joe, 98
Singleton, James W., 24
Slater, Mrs., 57, 178
Sleichmann, John, 93
Smith, General Kirby, 11, 87
Sons of Liberty, 23
Spangler, Edward (Ned), 57, 93, 98–99, 101, 114, 152, 165
Stanton, Edwin M., U.S. Secretary of War, 5, 41–42, 61–62, 66, 68, 71, 73, 82, 103–105, 111, 137, 154–157, 160, 166, 168, 170, 172–176, 182
Star Saloon, 95, 115
Stephens, Alexander, 64, 85
Stevens, Thaddeus, 75, 153
Steward, Joseph B., 117
Stewart, Dr. Richard H., 140–141, 142
Sumner, Senator Charles, 34–35, 74
Surratt, John Harrison, Jr. (alias John Watson): assassination preparations, 92–93, 123; as conspirator, 55–59, 91, 158, 160, 162, 165–168, 183–184; as courier, 9–10, 80, 82, 86; escape of, 151, 152, 155, 169–172, 174–175; plot to kidnap Lincoln, 68–71; trial of, 176, 177–182
Surratt, Mrs. Mary Eugenia, 55, 56–57, 58–60, 70, 92–93, 98, 101–102, 123, 137, 150–151, 152, 155–168, 170, 172, 173–174, 175, 176, 181, 183

Index

Surratt's Tavern, 83, 123–128, 164
Swann, Oscar, 131–132

Taft, Dr. Charles, 5–6
Taltavul, Peter, 115; *see also* Star Saloon
Thompson, Jacob, 21–22, 24–25, 27, 36, 39, 42–43, 55, 73, 78, 80, 86, 158–159, 178, 184
Tucker, Beverly, 20–21, 158

Union, 34–36, 39, 44, 76, 104, 157; the Army of the, 17, 18, 35, 37, 38, 68, 73, 83

Vallandigham, Clement L., 22–25
Victoria, Queen, *see* Great Britain

Watson, John, *see* Surratt, John

Weichmann, Louis J., 55–56, 58–59, 69, 70, 80, 92, 93, 101–102, 151, 155–156, 161–162, 163–164
Welles, Gideon, U.S. Secretary of the Navy, 110
White, Dr., 111
Wilderness, Battle of the, 69, 87
Wilkes, John, 46
Willard's Hotel, 15
Winter Garden Theater, 54
Winter, William, 49
Withers, Professor William, 114, 117
Wood, Lewis, *see* Powell, Lewis
Wyndham, Sir Charles, 49–50

Young, Bennett, 39–40, 68, 73, 76
Young, George, 158

About the Author

LARRY STARKEY received his first writing award as a junior in an Ohio high school, and, since earning a bachelor's degree in history and political science, has been a writer for the last fifteen years. He lives and works in Manhattan, and *Wilkes Booth Came to Washington* is his first published book.